P9-DHM-679

Barbarians to Angels

Also by Peter S. Wells

The Battle That Stopped Rome:
Emperor Augustus, Arminius, and the Slaughter of the Legions in the Teutoburg Forest

Barbarians to Angels

The Dark Ages Reconsidered

Peter S. Wells

❖

❖

W · W · Norton & Company

New York London

Printed in the United States of America

Book design by Margaret M. Wagner
Production manager: Julia Druskin

ISBN 978-0-393-06075-1

W. W. Norton & Company, Inc.
500 Fifth Avenue, New York, N.Y. 10110

W. W. Norton & Company Ltd.
Castle House, 75/76 Wells Street, London W1T 3QT

Book Club Edition

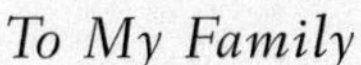

To My Family

Contents

❖

Preface

❖

IN NORTH AMERICA AND EUROPE, WE TRACE THE development of our societies through the ancient Greeks and Romans, the Renaissance, the Enlightenment, the Industrial Revolution, and into the twentieth and twenty-first centuries. But there is one period that seems to represent a major break in this story of progressive emergence of civilization—the Dark Ages that followed the glories of the Roman Empire. Many of our ideas about "barbarians"—illiterate and violent peoples who invade, loot, and pillage civilized communities—come from descriptions by late Roman writers of groups they called Alamanni, Franks, Goths, and Huns. Our popular understanding of the centuries that followed the decline of the Roman Empire—from A.D. 400 to 800—depends largely on the picture of barbarian invaders that Edward Gibbon presented in his *History of the Decline and Fall of the Roman Empire*, published more than two hundred years ago.

Gibbon portrayed Roman civilization in glorious terms:

> In the second century of the Christian era, the empire of Rome comprehended the fairest part of the earth, and the most civilised portion of mankind. The frontiers of that extensive monarchy were guarded by ancient renown and disciplined valour. The gentle, but powerful, influence of laws and manners had gradually cemented the union of the provinces. Their peaceful inhabitants enjoyed and abused the advantages of wealth and luxury. The image of a free constitution was preserved with decent reverence. The Roman senate appeared to possess the sovereign authority, and devolved on the emperors all the executive powers of government. During a happy period of more than fourscore years, the public administration was conducted by the virtue and abilities of Nerva, Trajan, Hadrian, and the two Antonines.
>
> Among the innumerable monuments of architecture constructed by the Romans, how many have escaped the notice of history, how few have resisted the ravages of time and barbarism! And yet even the majestic ruins that are still scattered over Italy and the provinces would be sufficient to prove that those countries were once the seat of a polite and powerful empire.

Thus Gibbon presents the Roman Empire of the late first and second centuries as a cultural and political paradise.

He then goes on to describe the ravages of the Goths, Vandals, Huns, and other "barbarian" peoples who brought a violent end to this near-perfect world.

> The haughty Rhodogast . . . marched from the northern extremities of Germany almost to the gates of Rome, and left the remains of his army to achieve the destruction of the West. The Vandals, the Suevi, and the Burgundians formed the strength of this mighty host; . . . the Alani . . . added their active cavalry to the heavy infantry of the Germans . . . and the Gothic adventurers. . . . Twelve thousand warriors, distinguished . . . by their noble birth or their valiant deeds, glittered in the van; and the whole multitude, which was not less than two hundred thousand fighting men, might be increased by the accession of women, of children, and of slaves, to the amount of four hundred thousand persons.

Such images of teeming hordes of barbarians descending on the civilized world of Rome formed the basis of many people's ideas about the fall of the Empire and the beginning of the chaos that followed.

According to this view, accepted by many who read and admired Gibbon's great historical work, only with Charlemagne about the year A.D. 800 did European societies again strive to attain the cultural achievements of the Romans. Charlemagne's policies fostered the spread of literacy, the rebirth of Roman-style architecture, and a renewed flourishing of learning and the arts. From Charlemagne and the Holy Roman Empire, we can trace a more-or-less direct line to the Renaissance and modern times.

But there is a fundamental problem with this picture of a four-hundred-year gap in which barbarism prevailed, and this book presents a different perspective on the period. The idea of the Dark Ages is a historical relic from the time when texts were the only source of information about the past, and no one understood the archaeological evidence well enough to use it to fill the gap. By "texts" I mean the information that was recorded by writers of the time—such as St. Jerome and St. Patrick in the fifth century, Gregory of Tours in the sixth, and Bede in the eighth—and has survived as original manuscripts or in later copies. As we shall see, these writings were strongly biased toward a Rome-centric view of the world.

We now have the benefit of archaeological material from the first millennium, which is rich enough to give us a powerful alternative picture. As I show in this book, the time once known as the Dark Ages—the fifth through eighth centuries—was anything but dark. It was a time of brilliant cultural activity. Only writers who believed that Rome and its society and values constituted the ideals of human existence viewed succeeding centuries as a period of decline and darkness. If we focus on the material evidence that the peoples of temperate Europe left behind, instead of on the rantings of late Roman writers about societies they did not understand, we see a creative and dynamic picture of these centuries emerge. Subsequent developments in Europe, including the Renaissance and modern civilization, owe as much to the "barbarians" as to Rome. Rather than a disjuncture in cultural life, the fifth, sixth, seventh, and eighth centuries—the "Dark Ages" to some—were times during which Europeans created the basis for medieval and modern Western civilization.

The title of this book has significance on two levels. "Barbarians to Angels" represents the major change in our understanding of the period known as the Dark Ages, from one based on late Roman written sources that portray the time as one of violence and chaos, to a largely archaeologically based perspective that highlights the significant cultural achievements of the period. The title derives from two works that emphasize very different perspectives on the people who lived during the fifth through eighth centuries. In *The History of the Decline and Fall of the Roman Empire*, Gibbon referred to "the ravages of . . . barbarism." When Gerald of Wales saw illuminated Biblical texts in Ireland, such as those discussed in chapter 12, this twelfth-century writer observed that these extraordinary artistic products must be "the work of angels."

Barbarians to Angels

1
Between Antiquity and the Middle Ages: What Happened?

❖

THE GLORIOUS CIVILIZATION OF THE ROMAN EMPIRE collapsed in the fifth century. After a period of cultural barbarism known as the Dark Ages, Europe finally re-created civilization around A.D. 800 with the rise of Charlemagne, with the Carolingian Renaissance, and with the establishment of the Holy Roman Empire. This is the traditional, and in some minds still the accepted, view of the formation of European civilization in the first millennium.

The intervening period between the peak of Roman power and the emergence of the Carolingian kingdom, A.D. 400–800, has been understood as the antithesis of these two culturally rich civilizations, with decline taking place in all important aspects of cultural life. Literacy declined, with fewer and fewer people able to read and write. Cities were abandoned and fell into ruin as people deserted the impoverished urban centers and fled to the countryside. With the collapse of Roman political authority, marauding bands of barbarian warriors looted and pillaged wherever they wanted to, because the rule of law had withered away and few local armed forces could withstand the assaults. Fine manufactures such as factory-made terra sigillata pottery and elegant painted glassware faded from the scene, to be replaced by crude handmade wares produced in scruffy settlements. Without Roman control of the seas and overland highways, trade collapsed and communities became cut off from the larger world.

This idea about what happened after the fall of the Roman Empire is vividly portrayed by Piranesi in his etchings of Roman ruins, made about the same time that Gibbon was writing his great history. Piranesi's views show partly collapsed stone temples, arches, and theaters, their foundations buried in accumulated sediments and their fragmentary walls overgrown with vegetation. Amid the ruins we see a few people, usually raggedly dressed and often tending cattle or sheep. What these images tell us is that after Rome collapsed, nothing remotely comparable followed in its footsteps to carry the banner of civilization. Such was the eighteenth-century view of the fall of the Roman Empire. This set of ideas about Rome, its collapse, and subsequent developments have dominated popular understanding to the present day.

This book challenges this picture. The traditional model of the development of European culture and society during the first millennium is based almost exclusively on the surviving texts—documents by Roman writers in the third, fourth, and fifth centuries, and by the few writers who were active during the sixth, seventh, and early eighth centuries, such as Gregory of Tours in France and Bede in England. From the point of view of such writers, and historians who use their writings as their primary sources of information, these centuries between 400 and 800 were indeed "dark"—there is not much written information about them.

But a very different story now emerges from the abundant archaeological evidence that is available for this period from all parts of Europe. Using that evidence, I show that there was no gap in cultural development between the Roman Empire and the Carolingian Renaissance. There were certainly major changes, but to judge them in terms of "decline," or the communities that instigated the changes as "barbaric," is to adopt the cultural prejudices of the late Roman writers. What has traditionally been called the Dark Ages was a period of immense cultural, economic, and political development along lines different from those of Roman civilization as we traditionally understand it.

Most people have an idea about what the Roman Empire was like from reading books about it, seeing films and television programs concerning Rome, or visiting Roman sites in Europe, North Africa, and Asia. In many different lands that had been part of the Roman Empire, immense structures built during the imperial period still stand—for example, in Rome, London, Cologne, Paris, and Vienna. Museums throughout Europe, as well as many in North America, display the products of mass production of Roman factories, including the bright reddish-orange pottery known as terra sigillata, bronze wine-serving vessels, and painted glassware. Many readers are familiar with Roman writers such as Caesar, Livy, and Tacitus, whose surviving texts tell of the glories of Roman civilization. Major cities hold constant reminders of Roman architecture and art. Government and university buildings, banks, and schools often are designed from Roman models. Statues of prominent political figures, war heroes, and popular icons are often crafted in the style of Roman sculpture.

Our modern ideas about Rome can be traced back to the Enlightenment of the eighteenth century, when serious study of ancient civilizations began. Throughout the nineteenth century, as the learned public became interested in large questions about human progress and history, images of Roman decline held great fascination. Especially for the wealthy and well-educated practitioners of history, natural science, and other scholarly endeavors, Greek and Roman civilization occupied a special place in the imagination. The young men from these social classes were trained in the classical languages and the history of the classical lands. The Grand Tour, a tradition among British and continental aristocracies during the eighteenth and nineteenth centuries, brought wealthy young men into direct contact with the stone architecture of the ancient Mediterranean societies. Piranesi's (1720–1778) etchings were popular and widely circulated images of the once glorious Roman past, now in ruins.

These visual images, coupled with texts by the late Roman writers, provided models for popular and scholarly understanding of the end of Roman civilization in the fifth and sixth centuries. The names of the barbarian peoples of this period—Visigoths and Ostrogoths, Alamanni, Burgundians, Franks, Saxons, Langobards, Alans, Gepids, and Huns—conjure up images of savagery and destruction. The name Vandals designates wanton destruction in our own time.

Rome was at its height of economic and political success in the first and second centuries. During the third century, a series of crises changed everything, and the Roman Empire was never again as mighty. Barbarian invaders from the north and east, whom Roman writers called Alamanni, crossed the *limes* boundary into Roman imperial territory. Economic problems threatened the stability of the Empire. Many peoples beyond the frontiers of the Empire began to pose military threats against Rome. Although the traditionally accepted dates for the fall of the Roman Empire are in the fifth century, after the third century the Empire did not expand any further, the building of monumental structures effectively ceased, and Rome came to rely increasingly on mercenaries hired from beyond its frontiers to guard the weakening borders.

The gradual pace of decline from the middle of the third century is punctuated in our understandings of the period by the late Roman texts that tell of horrific events precipitated by invading bands of warriors.

> The . . . Huns . . . exceed every degree of savagery . . . They are subject to no royal restraint, but they are content with the disorderly government of their important men, and led by them they force their way through every obstacle . . . they . . . divide suddenly into scattered bands and attack, rushing about in disorder here and there, dealing terrific slaughter . . . you would not hesitate to call them the most terrible of all warriors. . . . In truces they are faithless and unreliable . . . sacrificing every feeling to the mad impulse of the moment. Like unreasoning beasts, they are utterly ignorant of the difference between right and wrong. . . . (Ammianus Marcellinus, A.D. 380s)

> I shudder when I think of the calamities of our time. For twenty years the blood of Romans has been shed daily between Constantinople and the Alps. . . . these regions have been sacked and pillaged by Goths and Alans, Huns and Vandals. How many noble and virtuous women have been made the sport of these beasts! . . . the Roman world is falling. . . . Rome's army, once the lord of the world, trembles today at sight of the foe. (St. Jerome, about A.D. 410).

Four hundred years later, Charlemagne was embarking on a program of monumental architecture and political integration. Charlemagne's Royal Chapel at Aachen is just one of many signs of the large-scale building projects that characterize the

Figure 1.1. Aachen Cathedral, view looking south. The central part, with octagonal shape and dome, contains the original chapel built for Charlemagne in the late eighth century. The rest of the structure, most of it in Gothic style, was added during the later Middle Ages.

Carolingian Renaissance of the late eighth and early ninth centuries. It was the largest church building north of the Alps when it was constructed, and it still forms the nucleus of Aachen Cathedral, which was expanded during the Gothic period. Many other signs of integration of large-scale political power and programs of monumental building make clear that this new grand scale of physical expression was part of much larger developments that were under way. Attached by a covered walkway to the Royal Chapel was the monumental hall that Charlemagne had built as the political center of his realm. This palace was in the form of a basilica, a rectangular space 155 feet long and 68 feet wide with an apse at one end. It borrowed its form from northern European and Roman precedents (chapter 3).

Other palaces, cathedrals, and monasteries further attest to the grandiose building plans of Charlemagne and his successors. The much-studied design of the monastery of St. Gall in Switzerland reflects this new grandiosity of architectural vision. Charlemagne had a great bridge, said to have been five hundred paces in length, built over the Rhine at Mainz. Charlemagne's "big thinking" is further illustrated by his enormous construction project, the planned digging of a canal to connect the North Sea and the Rhineland with the Danube River provinces of central Europe. Work on this project, started in 793 by an army of diggers, had only begun when the soldiers laboring on the effort were called away to more pressing matters. (The first several hundred yards of the great ditch dug by the troops survive in a village in Bavaria, Germany, appropriately named Graben, meaning "canal" or "ditch.")

Large-scale construction projects of the late eighth and early ninth centuries were not limited to Charlemagne's vision alone; they indicate a much broader change under way throughout western and northern Europe. The great wall extending 149 miles between England and Wales, known as Offa's Dyke, was built at this time, as was the Danevirke, an earthen wall 30 feet wide and 6 feet high across the southern end of Jutland, which once separated Denmark and Germany. In central Ireland, an enormous bridge, 525 feet long, built of oak timbers, was constructed at Clonmacnoise about A.D. 804 (a date ascertained from tree rings in surviving posts).

These examples from Charlemagne's capital at Aachen and other parts of northern and western Europe represent a wide-reaching change throughout the continent during the Carolingian period of the late eighth and early ninth centuries. The new monumentality of construction—of churches and cathedrals, of palaces, boundary walls, and bridges—indicates that individuals of considerable political and economic power were once again emerging. Only power and authority that reached well beyond individual communities could command the resources, expertise, and labor effort required to build these great structures. Charlemagne's concern with re-creating symbols of Rome—in the structure of his chapel, the form of his governmental palace, his fostering of Latin literacy, and many aspects of the visual arts—provides a coherent close to the period known as the Dark Ages.

But what actually happened during the intervening period between the height of Roman power and the rise of Charlemagne? Was it the time of unremitting barbarity and chaos that many late Roman commentators would have us believe? Or were important developments under way that determined the nature of the Carolingian rebirth and were necessary for the rise of that new society?

As we shall see in the following chapters, Charlemagne and his innovations did not appear suddenly at the end of the eighth century. They were part of a whole series of economic, social, and political developments from the fifth century on that archaeological evidence reveals to us even when written sources say little about them. These changes form the basis for the chapters that follow.

Of fundamental importance was the development of a new technology of agriculture—the moldboard plow—which vastly increased the efficiency of food production beyond anything in Roman times. This new technology meant that fewer people could produce larger harvests than was possible earlier, thereby releasing many former farmers to work in other, specialized, activities such as manufacturing, trade, and building.

During the "Dark Ages," innovations in architecture led to the emergence of the familiar cathedral of the High Middle Ages. An architectural historian has written recently that during the period 565–800, "medieval architecture was born."

Crafts workers created a new style of art during this period. It was expressed on personal ornaments such as gold brooches and intricate belt decorations, in exquisite chalices for churches all over Europe, in the illuminated manuscripts of Celtic Britain and Ireland, and in the decorations on ship prows and church facades throughout the continent.

Despite the term "Dark Ages," a number of important historians were active during these centuries. They include Jordanes writing his history of the Goths in the sixth century, Gregory of Tours documenting the Franks during that same century, and Bede recording the history of England in the early eighth century.

If formal education faltered in Italy and some other former lands of the Empire, it thrived elsewhere, especially in Ireland. During the sixth century, Columba founded his internationally famous center of learning at Iona. Columbanus, educated in Ireland, left to establish monasteries and schools on the continent, bringing with him a whole new tradition of learning.

With the breakdown of Roman political organization in the provinces, Roman law ceased to be enforced. But each new national community created its own code of laws, partly based on the Roman system but always with distinctive features that grew out of their own traditions. Frankish, Irish, and Anglo-Saxon law codes were written down in the course of the sixth century.

Most importantly, all of these developments grew out of the local traditions of the peoples of temperate Europe, including the Franks, Anglo-Saxons, and Goths. The experience of Roman rule had had an effect, but the new civilization that emerged with Charlemagne was distinctively European, not Mediterranean.

The following chapters explore these developments.

2
The Decline of the Roman Empire

❖

TO UNDERSTAND THE SIGNIFICANCE OF THE DEVELopments that form the focus of this book—the cultural, economic, and social changes of the period A.D. 400–800—we need to review briefly what we know about the decline, disintegration, and ultimate collapse of the Roman Empire.

THE ROMAN EMPIRE

The origins of Rome go back at least to the late Bronze Age, around 1200 B.C., when farming villages occupied the hills that later played such important roles in the topography of the great city. During the sixth century B.C., the growing center—at the time under the domination of the Etruscans—engaged actively in trade with Greek colonies in southern parts of Italy.

The year 510 B.C. is the traditional date for the beginning of the Roman Republic, when Rome emerged from Etruscan rule and became an independent city. Around the middle of the third century B.C., Rome began its territorial expansion in the coastal lands of the Mediterranean Sea. Major conquests north of the Alps in Europe began with Julius Caesar's wars in Gaul (modern France and other lands west of the Rhine) between 58 and 51 B.C. In 27 B.C., Augustus was named the first emperor of Rome, and from this time on we speak of the "Roman Empire." Other territorial additions to the Empire followed, such as conquest of lands south of the Danube River in 15 B.C., and the invasion of Britain in A.D. 43 and the conquest of most of the island in the following years.

The first two centuries A.D. were, for most of the Roman Empire, the peak of peace and prosperity. (In Britain, many regions thrived economically into the fourth century.) During these centuries, most of the stone and brick architecture that survives today was constructed, the majority of what are considered the greatest artworks were created, and Latin literature flourished. Roman engineers designed and built roads throughout the Empire to enable troops to move quickly over all types of terrain. When the roads were not used by the soldiers, merchants and others could travel on them to expedite their journeys. Workers built foundations for the roads that consisted of layers of gravel and sand, then paved them with flat stones. The road surface was higher than the surrounding land, and the pavement was highest at the center, so rainwater would run off and the surface would stay dry. Stone bridges, often with expansive arches, carried roads over streams and rivers. Roman bridges were built so solidly that many are still in use to carry traffic today.

Although roads all over the Empire bore considerable traffic in trade goods, bulk commodities such as grain, wine, and

Figure 2.1. Places mentioned in chapters 2, 3, and 4.

olive oil were shipped in great volumes by boat, especially in the Mediterranean but also in the North Sea and along the major rivers. Before the invention of motorized vehicles during the Industrial Revolution, waterborne transport was much less costly than overland travel. Pottery, bronze ornaments, glass vessels, and iron tools were traded locally and over great dis-

Figure 2.2. Hadrian's Wall. Constructed mostly between A.D. 120 and 140, it runs across what is now northern England from the Irish Sea to the North Sea. It marked the northwestern boundary of the Roman Empire. This view, looking east, is from the Roman fort at Housesteads.

tances. Where water transport was not available or loads were small, trade goods could be carried by wagons on the roads or by human porters bearing packs on their backs. Bronze, silver, and gold coins provided standards of value for trade, and these are found today throughout the former lands of the Roman Empire and even in places beyond the imperial frontiers where people traded with the Roman world.

In some parts of their Empire, such as Europe north of the Alps, Roman builders introduced stone and brick architecture where wood and clay plaster had formerly been the essential materials for constructing houses and other buildings. Aqueducts were built of stone or brick to bring freshwater into Roman cities and towns. Although the majority of people got their drinking and washing water from public fountains, wealthy Romans often had running water coming into their houses through pipes connected to the main urban supply. Wastewater flowed out of the cities through underground sewers constructed of stone and brick. Many wealthy Romans had central heating in their city houses and country villas. Under the floor was an open area that was heated by a firebox in the basement. The heated air warmed the floors, and flues in the walls allowed hot air to flow up through the walls, warming them.

As the Roman Empire expanded through territorial conquest, Roman law was introduced into the provinces. The Roman tradition of a written code of law goes back to the XII Tables, which are believed to have been written in 451 and 450 B.C. What had been customary law before that, based on the tradition of the community, from this point on became formal statute. Although law evolved over the centuries in response to political and social changes, Romans believed that their law's basic principles derived from that original code committed to text in the mid-fifth century B.C. The greatest development of thinking and writing about Roman law took place in the second century A.D., at the same time that the Empire was at its greatest size. The standardization of legal procedure that Roman law represented meant that a common system of practice existed, in theory at least, throughout the Empire. Roman law had important influences on the subsequent legal codes that developed among newly emergent societies during the post-Roman centuries.

ROME'S DECLINE

Rome thus rose to become the greatest power in the world during the five centuries after 500 B.C., and it thrived at its peak of territorial extent, population, wealth, and artistic and political achievement for the next two centuries. It is important to remember, however, that not everything was rosy for everyone during these times. Roman society was highly stratified, with wealthy landowning citizens at the top of the social pyramid and slaves at the bottom. Almost all governmental positions were held by wealthy men, and the legal system favored them in the law codes. Some slaves were able to gain their freedom and become wealthy, but the majority of them remained bound to their owners for life. In the provinces, citizens from Rome often administered local governments, but it was Roman policy to coopt indigenous elites to serve in the administration of provincial affairs. We know that there were rebellions and civil wars in Italy, most notably in the two decades after the murder of Julius Caesar in 44 B.C. There were surely many uprisings and brutal retaliations in the provinces as well, probably many more than are recorded.

The decline ("collapse" is too strong a term) of the Roman Empire was a long, gradual process that took place over at least three centuries. Looked at from a modern perspective, it can seem like a steady, even inevitable unraveling of the military, political, and economic institutions that Rome had created over its seven centuries of growth. But it was much more complex than that, and few people living at the time would have noticed or felt that their world was declining. In different parts of the vast Roman Empire, changes occurred at different times, and often a period of apparent decline would be followed by one of renewed growth.

Because the events and processes that characterize the decline of Rome happened at different times and in different ways in different regions, it is impossible to point to a single event that marks the end of the Empire. The Empire—if by that term we mean the entire political, military, economic, and cultural complex of institutions and practices that characterized Rome—faded and petered out; it did not simply end. Certain events have been noted as signaling the end of Roman power. Alaric's conquest with his Gothic army of Rome in A.D. 410 is often cited as a convenient marker for the end of the Empire. Another date often cited is A.D. 476, when the first emperor of Germanic origin—Odoacer—rose to rule over the western part of the Empire from the capital at Ravenna in Italy.

The following brief and oversimplified summary will convey the complexity of the events that played parts in the decline. My emphasis here is on the western, rather than the eastern, part of the Empire.

By the final third of the second century A.D., there were clear indications of serious threats to the peace and prosperity that had reigned in the provinces for nearly two centuries. Written sources tell of a series of invasions by tribal groups across the upper and middle Danube River into the Roman provinces. Known as the Marcomannic Wars, these invasions took place between A.D. 166 and 180. They are named for the tribe known as the Marcomanni, but other groups, including the Quadi and the Iazyges (a Sarmatian people), participated as well. The texts tell us that the invaders crossed the Danube, attacked Roman military bases and killed and wounded soldiers, and pillaged civilian settlements.

The third century A.D. was one of crisis throughout much of the Roman Empire. Some of the problems were internal to the workings of the Empire, including inflation and the resulting difficulties paying for essential governmental services, such as soldiers' wages. Other problems were related directly to difficulties on the frontiers. With increasing stress created by Alamanni, Franks, Goths, and other groups on the frontiers on the Rhine and Danube, for example, many people moved away from the border regions of the provinces to escape the attacks. The abandonment of numerous communities exacerbated the problems, creating agricultural shortages in lands upon which troops depended for their sustenance. Thus a whole series of interrelated problems developed, all ultimately resulting from stresses precipitated by the overextension of the Empire and the growing political and military power of groups beyond the frontiers.

The emperors Valerian (A.D. 253–260) and his son Gallienus (253–268) attempted to deal with these problems (Valerian and his adult son ruled together as emperors from 253 to 260; after 260, Gallienus ruled alone until 268). Under their leadership, the Roman frontier along the *limes* boundary in southwestern Germany was retracted to create a more easily defensible border. The corner of land between the upper Rhine and upper Danube rivers was given up, and a new border was created along the upper reaches of those two rivers.

Written sources tell of major raids beginning in A.D. 259 by Germanic groups east of the Rhine across the lower Rhine near Cologne. Parties of the invaders surged through Gaul and into Spain. At about the same time, other Germanic peoples raided across the Danube River and over the eastern Alps into Italy. The Roman frontier troops were ever less able to hinder—let alone stop—these incursions. In what seems to us an odd twist, many of the Germanic warriors who were captured, often as they traveled back toward their homelands across the frontiers, were recruited to serve in the Roman border forces. This process had, of course, a major impact on the composition and cultural character of these forces.

Figure 2.3. Reconstructed wooden watchtower on the *limes* at Hienheim, Bavaria, in southern Germany. Such watchtowers were manned by teams of about ten Roman soldiers. On the ground floor was the kitchen, on the second floor the living and sleeping room, and on the top floor the guard station. Such towers were built all along the *limes* boundary, from the middle Rhine in the west to the upper Danube in the east.

For the next several decades, the peoples who inhabited lands beyond the frontiers made many successful incursions into Roman provincial territory, but sometimes Roman military forces were able to repel them. When Diocletian became emperor in A.D. 284, he began to reorganize the administration of the provinces. In 293 he established a Tetrarchy of four

Figure 2.4. Portchester Castle, on the English Channel coast of southern England. This fortress was originally built late in the third century, and it remains one of the best-preserved Roman forts in Europe. It was used for defensive purposes in later times as well, but it preserves much of its original architecture.

emperors: himself and Galerius to administer the eastern part of the Empire, and Maximinus and Constantius the western part. At this stage, Rome ceased to be the political capital of the Empire. Instead, four new regional capitals were established—at Milan (in northern Italy), Sirmium (near Belgrade in Serbia), Nicomedia (Izmit in Turkey), and Trier (in western Germany). Under Diocletian and the Tetrarchy, a new phase of fort construction along all of the frontiers of the Empire was undertaken.

After Diocletian and Maximinus retired in 305, the Roman Empire plunged into civil war for two decades. When Constantius died in York in 306, the army stationed there proclaimed his son Constantine the new emperor. In 312, at the

Figure 2.5. Palace of Constantine in Trier, western Germany. This enormous building, constructed of brick between A.D. 305 and 310, illustrates the monumental scale on which Rome built in its provinces, even in this relatively late period. At a total height of 118 feet, it towers over the surrounding buildings in the modern city. It is 233 feet long and 107 feet wide, and the walls are nine feet thick.

battle of the Milvian Bridge (in Rome), Constantine's army defeated the forces under Maxentius to win sole emperorship of the western part of the Roman Empire. Some accounts suggest that Constantine fought the battle with divine inspiration from the new religion Christianity. In 324 Constantine met and defeated the army of Licinius and conquered the city of Byzantium (subsequently Constantinople, now Istanbul) to become sole emperor of Rome.

After Constantine's death in 337, new fighting broke out for the position of emperor. At the same time, battles were occurring regularly between Roman forces and their opponents on both sides of the Rhine and Danube rivers. In the early

350s, Roman troops suffered a number of serious defeats in the Rhine valley, but in the late 350s Roman leaders achieved some success. In the Battle of Strasbourg in 357, Roman forces under Julian defeated a major army of Alamannic soldiers. In the late 360s, defenses along the west bank of the Rhine were restrengthened, culminating in a final building program in 369. In the 380s, the Roman emperor Valentinian II appointed a Frank as field general in the west, the first instance of a Germanic military leader in the Roman army. At the Battle of Adrianople, in the lower Danube region, in 378, a large army of Goths soundly defeated the Roman general Valens and his 15,000 to 30,000 troops, paving the way for Goths and their allies to move across the frontier into the provinces, thereby forever changing the political and cultural character of this important part of the Empire.

After the emperor Theodosius's death in 395, the Roman Empire was divided into an eastern and a western part (making official a division that had long existed in practice). The Vandal Stilicho ruled the western half from 395 to 408. From this point on, Germanic and other non-Roman soldiers played ever-increasing roles in the army of the late Empire. Stilicho negotiated with representatives of the Alamanni and Franks in 396, establishing contracts with them to ensure their cooperation. Peace reigned on the Rhine until 406. When Alaric and his Goths threatened Italy in 401, Stilicho brought in troops from Britain and the Rhineland to confront him. Stilicho was successful, and he took on Alaric as military adviser.

In the years 406 and 407, a massive series of armies said to consist of Alans, Pannonians, Suebi, and Vandals crossed southern Germany and the Rhine into Gaul, plundering cities and towns on an unprecedented scale. The date 406 is often considered the time of the official end of Roman protection on the Rhine. Then in 410, what had been a political understanding between Alaric, leader of the Gothic army, and the Roman senate disintegrated, and Alaric led his troops in an attack on Rome. His soldiers sacked the city. That same year, Roman military leaders struggling to ward off invaders from northern Britain, Ireland, and the shores of the continent requested military assistance from Rome, but they were (of course) denied the support. Hence this year—410—is frequently cited as the date for the "end of Roman Britain." But, as noted above, this designation is arbitrary. Though Rome could not send any new troops, the cultural and political character of Britain did not change overnight.

In one of the last major confrontations between what was left of the Roman armies and their Germanic allies, a huge force of Roman troops from contingents stationed in Gaul and Italy, together with allied Burgundians and Visigoths, met an army said by commentators of the time to have numbered in the hundreds of thousands and commanded by Attila, emperor of the Huns. Attila had created a great military power in central Europe, based on the Hungarian Plain, that was made up of once-nomadic horse-riding peoples from central Asia together with numerous Germanic groups from eastern Europe. Attila's power was so great, and Rome feared Hunnic invasion so much, that Rome paid him subsidies—protection money—to stay away from the provinces. This sum reached the stunning amount of 2,100 pounds of gold for the year 447. A description of Attila survives, recorded by the historian Jordanes, perhaps originally written by Priscus.

> He [Attila] was haughty in his carriage, casting his eyes about him on all sides so that the proud man's power was to be seen in the very movements of his body. A lover of war,

> he was personally restrained in action, most impressive in counsel, gracious to suppliants, and generous to those to whom he had once given his trust. He was short of stature with a broad chest, massive head, and small eyes.

Priscus's description of a banquet conveys a sense of the special ways in which Attila distinguished himself.

> While sumptuous food had been prepared—served on silver platters—for the other barbarians and for us, for Attila there was nothing but meat on a wooden trencher. He showed himself temperate in all other ways too, for gold and silver goblets were offered to the men at the feast, but his mug was of wood. His dress too was plain . . . nor was the sword by his side, nor the clasps of his barbarian boots, nor the bridle of his horse, like those of other Scythians, adorned with gold or gems or anything of high price.

After conquering and pillaging widely in the eastern part of Europe, Attila led his troops, which included a number of different peoples, westward through what is now Germany, across the Rhine, and into France toward Paris. The Roman troops and their west Germanic allies, all under the command of the military governor in the west, Aetius, confronted Attila's massed horde in a great battle in a place recorded as the Catalaunian Fields, the location of which is not known today. Accounts of the time indicate that 165,000 soldiers were killed, but modern researchers regard this number as vastly inflated. The significance of this event is that it was the last of the major battles between what can reasonably be called a "Roman" army and non-Roman forces in Europe.

Many historians feel that the end of the western Roman

Empire occurred in 476, not as the result of a momentous battle but with the emergence of a king of probable Germanic origin—Odoacer—as the last western Roman emperor, based at the fifth-century capital in Ravenna, Italy. He recognized the eastern Roman Empire, based in Constantinople, as the true successor to the once-powerful Roman Empire of the first and second centuries. Rather than assuming the title of Emperor of the West, as he might have done, he had the symbols of the rank of emperor—the imperial cloak and crown—sent to Constantinople.

But yet another possible end date for the Roman Empire in the west might be proposed. In the middle of the sixth century, the eastern emperor Justinian launched campaigns in the lands bordering on the western Mediterranean—in Italy, Spain, and north Africa—reconquering some of those former parts of the Empire. With Justinian's death in 565, this last attempt to resurrect the old western Roman Empire came to an end.

While Roman rule was gradually disintegrating in Italy, throughout the Mediterranean basin, and in the provinces beyond the Alps, the peoples of Europe living in the former lands of the Empire and farther north beyond the old imperial frontiers were thriving.

3
The Peoples of Europe

❖

THE PEOPLES OF DARK AGE WESTERN EUROPE ARE known by names such as Alamanni, Angles, Burgundians, Franks, Frisians, Jutes, Saxons, Thuringians, and Visigoths. In the British Isles, the inhabitants are known as Irish, Picts, Scots, and, from the fourth century on, newly arrived Angles, Saxons, and Jutes. In eastern Europe were Slavs and groups thought to have migrated from farther east, such as Alans, Avars, Gepids, Goths, and Huns. Sorting out these different peoples, tracing their origins and movements, and learning how they changed over time are immensely complex tasks for which we have far too little information with which to work.

We know most of these names because late Roman and early Byzantine writers, such as Ammianus Marcellinus, Priscus, and Jordanes, recorded them. Few members of these groups were themselves literate; as a result, almost all of the accounts about them were written by people who did not belong to the groups they were describing. The situation is somewhat better with writers such as Gregory of Tours, a Frank himself, writing about the Franks in the middle of the sixth century. And when Bede wrote his history of England in the seventh century, he identified with the Anglo-Saxons, whose story he was telling. But of course these early writers understood the world very differently from the way we do today.

WHERE DID THEY COME FROM?

Where did all of these groups come from? Were they always where the commentators describe them, or did they move in from somewhere else? If they were always there, why do we first learn their names during the second or third centuries, as in the cases of Alamanni, Franks, and Goths, or as late as the sixth century, as in the cases of Slavs and Avars?

The first half of our period, A.D. 400–600, is known as the Migration period. Written accounts refer to large-scale migrations of peoples both outside and into the late Roman imperial territories, such as the movement of Alaric with his Gothic army that culminated in the sacking of Rome in 410. Migrations of the Alamanni, Burgundians, Franks, Goths, and others throughout the fifth and sixth centuries are seen as fundamental to the early formation of modern France and Germany. Invasions from the east by Goths, Alans, Huns, and Avars play similar roles in ideas about the origins of eastern European nations. For Britain, the migrations of Angles, Saxons, and Jutes during the fifth and sixth centuries have been fundamental to English peoples' perceptions of themselves and their relationships to continental Europeans.

How large were the migrations of the Migration period, how often did they occur, and what were they like? To address these questions, we need to consider critically the written sources about them and consult the archaeological evidence. In Greek and Roman ideas about ethnography, "barbarians"—a category to which all of the peoples mentioned above would have belonged—did not change. They remained the same over time, and had no "history," such as Greece and Rome did. From this perspective, it follows that changes observed by Romans among the peoples beyond their frontiers could be explained only by the arrival of new populations.

But scrutiny of the evidence suggests that many of the migrations that the writers mentioned did not take place in the way they are described in the written sources of the time. Instead, many accounts of migrations seem to have been created as origin myths to explain how a particular people came to live in and dominate a region. At the time when Rome was achieving its greatest power and influence, the poet Virgil (70–19 B.C.) wrote the story of Aeneas leaving the devastated city of Troy and journeying to Italy to found what was to become the great city of Rome. In early medieval times, several different groups, including the Franks and Lombards, adopted this Roman tradition and traced their own fictive origins to emigrants from Troy. A recent analysis of the long-accepted account of the migrations of the Goths from Scandinavia shows that it was a story created to serve a specific political purpose rather than record a real historical event. Elite groups created such migration myths to explain how they came to power (and why they should stay there).

I am not suggesting that movements of peoples did not occur at all, but that they rarely, if ever, involved the large numbers that many of the accounts indicate, especially in western and northern Europe. The archaeological evidence for migration there is sparse. If the stories recounted by the Dark Age writers were historically accurate, we would expect to find abundant material evidence for the arrival and settlement of new groups in different parts of Europe, with new types of houses, new styles of pottery and metalwork, and new burial practices. We would also expect to find evidence of abandonment in the areas from which people were supposed to have emigrated. But we do not find these patterns to any appreciable degree. Instead, the archaeological evidence indicates that the majority of people did not migrate. Small groups of elites, often with bands of their loyal warriors, sometimes moved from one region to another and quickly asserted their power over the peoples into whose land they moved. Such movements may have been recorded as "migration of Alamanni" or "immigration of Goths," but the reality was probably much smaller in scale.

CHANGING PERSPECTIVES: THE ANGLO-SAXONS

The idea of the migrations of Angles and Saxons from continental Europe to Britain during the Dark Ages will be familiar to most readers. The common picture is of waves of migrants from what are now northern Germany and Denmark, known by the names Angles, Saxons, and Jutes, sailing across the North Sea to invade southern England after the collapse of Roman power there at the beginning of the fifth century. Gildas in the sixth century wrote:

> A pack of cubs burst forth from the lair of the barbarian lioness . . . they would live for three hundred years in the land towards which their prows were directed, and . . . for half the time . . . they would repeatedly lay it waste.

❖

In the early eighth century, Bede, composing his history of the English people, relied on the work of Gildas and wrote of the *adventus Saxonum*—the coming of the Saxons—as a major event in British history. The story of King Arthur, and all of the themes of magic and supernatural powers associated with it, tie into this idea of the Saxon conquest of southern Britain. Arthur was supposedly a local leader in the western part of Britain, rallying his people against the invaders.

Until about thirty years ago, this idea of Angles and Saxons arriving on the shores of Britain from the continent, to replace the reduced post-Roman populations of the countryside, was generally accepted. Today, after three decades of systematic archaeological and natural scientific study, only a few scholars hold to this now antiquated model.

The fact is, there is little solid archaeological evidence for any migrations on a scale corresponding to the assertions of Gildas, Bede, and their successors. Scholars who have examined all of the relevant evidence from these centuries conclude that there is no indication of any kind of disjunction that reflects an abandonment of rural areas by post-Roman populations or indicates a massive new arrival of immigrants from outside. There has always been regular movement of people and goods between Britain and the continent, but not the mass migrations suggested by earlier investigators. New styles of pottery, brooches, and other objects are found on settlements and in cemeteries, but their appearance and the contexts in which they occur suggest that they were trade goods, objects of gift exchanges, or local products that were made in new styles adopted from other communities, rather than possessions brought by immigrant groups from across the sea.

Recent studies in the natural sciences support this view. Analyses of pollen samples show that the supposed great land-clearing that the immigrant Angles and Saxons undertook did not occur. The landscape of southern Britain had been substantially cleared of forest vegetation by the late Bronze Age, 1,500 years earlier, and it never regained the earlier state of woodland. Stable isotope analysis on teeth of individuals buried in typical "Anglo-Saxon" cemeteries in the north and south of England shows consistently that the individuals, whom earlier investigators would have interpreted as immigrants from the continent, were in fact local people.

MIGRATIONS IN EASTERN EUROPE

In parts of eastern Europe, the situation was somewhat different. Peoples known by names such as Alans, Avars, Gepids, and Huns seem to have migrated from far eastern Europe or western central Asia during these centuries, and many of them settled on or near the Hungarian Plain, perhaps because that environment was similar to the steppes of their homelands in western Asia. These groups are especially well represented by their strong emphasis on horse breeding and horseback riding, and their distinctive material culture, which included numerous metal ornaments attached to horses' harnesses. Other evidence for westward migration comes from the skeletons in graves.

The evidence is purposely shaped skulls on individuals buried in cemeteries in parts of eastern Europe, and in some instances farther westward. Characteristic are long, roughly conical shapes coming to almost a rounded point at the top. The practice of binding a baby's head with tight bands of cloth to cause the skull to assume an elongated shape was common among some peoples who lived north of the Black Sea. During the fifth and sixth centuries, such skulls are represented in cemeteries in several regions of Europe. In some cemeteries in the Carpathian basin, the majority of individuals buried in the graves had artificially shaped heads, as for example at Mözs, in southwestern Hungary, and at Gaweinstal, in lower Austria. We do not know whether the individuals in these graves were themselves immigrants from the east, or descendants of immigrants from the east, or possibly even local persons whose parents, for whatever reason, adopted this practice of head alteration. Cranial shaping can be carried out only on infants, when the skull is still soft enough to permit alteration.

In the sixth century, the names Slavs and Avars appear in Byzantine written sources. Peoples designated by these names played major roles in developments in the central regions of continental Europe during the succeeding centuries. Scholars now regard the Slavs not as a linguistically and culturally distinct group but instead as diverse peoples in eastern, central, and northern Europe who adopted social and political organization different from those that had been dominant earlier. The new societies were non-hierarchical and non-centralized, in contrast to those of the former Roman Empire and the existing Byzantine Empire, based in Constantinople. Characteristic of these Slavic groups are small settlements of modest wooden houses, plain handmade pottery, simple iron tools, and relatively few personal ornaments or imported objects.

Early in the sixth century, the group known as Avars arrived in central Europe from regions to the east. They were originally a horse-riding nomadic people, and their material culture is dominated by objects associated with horses. Numerous burials in which humans were accompanied by horses and ornate harness equipment have been found in a great many sixth-, seventh-, and eighth-century cemeteries in the Hungarian Plain and surrounding lands where written sources place the Avars. Other distinctive grave goods include iron stirrups, ornate belt buckles, lances, and complex bows made of wood, antler, and horn.

In the sixth, seventh, and eighth centuries, the lands north of the middle Danube, where the Czech Republic and Slovakia are now situated, were parts of an important frontier zone between the expanding Frankish Empire to the west and the Slavic and Avar peoples to the east. Farther east on the lower Danube, some communities that had practiced the nomadic Avar way of life gradually adopted agriculture in the latter part of the seventh century and eventually created what became the Bulgar Empire.

LIFEWAYS

Most of the people of Dark Age Europe were farmers. Agriculture and stock raising formed the basis of their economy and way of life. Most lived in small villages of houses built with timber frames and wattle-and-daub walls. The farmers grew mostly wheat, barley, and rye for their basic subsistence, along with legumes that included lentils and peas. They raised cattle, pigs, sheep, goats, horses, and dogs. In the forested regions and where natural pasturage was abundant, communities tended to raise more cattle and pigs; in less fertile areas, sheep and goats often predominated. Horses were raised especially for riding by elites and warriors. Besides cultivating crops and tending livestock, families worked at domestic crafts such as weaving woolen and linen textiles for clothing and making tools from wood, bone, and antler. A village potter made ceramic vessels that everyone needed for cooking and serving food, and a blacksmith forged and repaired tools such as plowshares, sickles, scythes, hammers, saws, axes, and knives. A specialist metalworker crafted bronze personal ornaments, such as decorative brooches and bracelets for women and belt buckles for men. The character of houses varied in different regions, and styles of pottery and metal tools and ornaments reflected local tastes and traditions. (Chapter 8 explores food production and village life in more detail.)

Cemeteries are an important source of information about the people of these centuries. Burial practice was by inhumation (not cremation), and grave goods were commonly arranged with the corpse. Women were commonly buried with personal ornaments such as brooches attached to their clothing and bracelets on their wrists, and some men were outfitted with iron weapons, most often lance heads and spearheads but sometimes swords, shields, and helmets. Pottery vessels were often placed in the graves of both women and men, and rich burials contained large quantities of imported pottery, bronze and even silver or gold vessels, and lavish ornaments of precious metal. Evidence from cemeteries enables us to understand status differences in communities and examine how the identity of individuals was expressed through the objects with which they were buried.

In northern Europe, ways of life were often different from those in most parts of the continent. In Ireland and Scotland, stock raising was often a major part of the subsistence pattern, with emphasis on cattle in some regions and sheep in others. Coastal communities exploited the sea, collecting shellfish and seabird eggs along the shores, and fishing and hunting seals from boats. In general, communities in these northwestern parts of Europe were smaller than those of the continent.

Several distinctive forms of settlement characterize Ireland

and Scotland. These include crannogs—farmsteads built on islands in lakes for protection. The islands could be natural or artificial, built up of stone and timber with soil brought in to pile on top. On the west coast of Scotland, some communities built *broch*s, round structures of drystone masonry (cut stone blocks fitted together without cement). Along the rocky coasts of Ireland and Scotland, large stone-walled forts were constructed. Excavations in some yield evidence for the manufacture of special items, such as fine bronze and silver metalwork for use by wealthy and powerful individuals, showing that these forts were political bases of elites—chieftains and local kings. Imported luxury goods indicate that these elites maintained trade contacts with places as far away as the Rhineland and even the eastern Mediterranean.

Figure 3.1. Crannog at Fair Head, County Antrim, Northern Ireland. This artificial island in the lake was constructed of stone, timber, and earth. A large number of crannogs are known in Ireland and Scotland, from prehistoric and especially early historic times.

RELIGION

In its earliest stages, Christianity was one of many cults that emerged in the lands along the eastern shores of the Mediterranean Sea. For the first three centuries A.D., most of what we know about the development of the new religion concerns that part of the world. Evidence for the spread of Christianity in our region of Europe first becomes clear early in the fourth century. Before that time, small groups of persons who practiced the new religion were resident in some of the late Roman cities, but it was not until the emperor Constantine converted to Christianity in the year 312 that persecution of Christians more or less stopped and Christianity began to be adopted throughout the provinces. One version of the story of Constantine's conversion tells that he believed that Christ had intervened on his behalf in the battle of the Milvian Bridge (chapter 2), and his victory convinced him that Christianity was the true religion. From the middle of the fourth century on, small churches were built in many regions of the imperial provinces, and cathedrals were erected in major Roman centers. From the fifth century, tombs of church officials became important ritual places for pilgrims and local families looking for holy places to bury their loved ones.

As Roman power waned in the European provinces, the practice of Christianity declined in many places, and beliefs and practices that had been prevalent earlier again became dominant. But missions dispatched by the popes in Rome introduced, or reintroduced, the new religion to the inhabitants of many parts of Europe. In 431, Palladius was sent to Ireland to bring Christianity there, and in the middle of that century St. Patrick labored for three decades to convert the Irish to the new religion. When the powerful Frankish king

Clovis adopted Christianity in the year 496—according to one account, because he, like Constantine, was convinced of Christ's ability to help him defeat his enemies—the way was open for the majority of Franks to adopt the faith (officially, at least). In 596 Pope Gregory sent St. Augustine (of Canterbury) to Britain to convert the Anglo-Saxons. Augustine succeeded in convincing the Saxon king Ethelbert of Kent (whose wife was already a Christian) to convert, and Canterbury became the center of Christianity in England. In most places that lay outside the former territories of the Roman Empire, conversion to Christianity happened much later (Ireland was an exception). In Denmark, for example, King Harald Bluetooth did not convert until about the year 960, and other parts of Scandinavia and the countries along the eastern and southern shores of the Baltic Sea converted even later.

We do not know much about religious beliefs in pre-Christian Europe except what we can glean from traditional sources that were written down later, such as myths and legends in Ireland (associated with names such as Belenos, Lug, and Macc Oc) and Scandinavia (Freya, Odin, Thor). But we do know a great deal about pre-Christian religious practices and rituals. Cult sites are common throughout pre-Christian Europe. Many are situated in places of outstanding natural character, such as on hilltops, at the confluence of streams, and on headlands with views out to sea. Ritual practice often involved making votive offerings of weapons, tools, jewelry, even human beings, to gods and spirits. Sometimes such offerings were buried in the ground, sometimes dropped into bodies of water, sometimes burned.

I explore some of the complex questions surrounding the spread of Christianity in more detail in chapter 11. Here I just make the point that, even when the leader of a community (such as the Roman emperor Constantine in 312, the Frankish king Clovis in 496, the Danish king Harald Bluetooth in 960) said that he has converted to Christianity, and his followers did—officially—as well, that does not mean that they suddenly started to believe things differently from the way they had before and gave up their traditional practices. As we shall see, people continued to practice their traditional rituals long after they had "officially" become Christian.

CONNECTIONS

We sometimes think of people in the past as living in small and isolated communities, cut off from the rest of the world. For the region in question, this was not the case. From the Neolithic period (beginning in 5000 B.C.) on, and certainly throughout the four centuries of our consideration here, virtually all communities were linked in networks along which goods, information, and ideas flowed. Chapter 10 looks at trade in some detail—long-distance commerce that linked Ireland with Egypt, central Sweden with Mesopotamia, and the more intensive local trade that brought people from different communities into contact on an almost daily basis. Trade enables people to acquire goods that they do not produce themselves, ranging from amber beads from the shores of the Baltic Sea to engraved silver bowls from Constantinople. The availability of goods through trade motivates people to work hard to produce surpluses that they can offer as exchange goods. And all trade includes the flow of information and ideas. Wherever there is evidence of trade, people were also exchanging ideas. Trade brought people into regular contact with their neighbors and traveling merchants. Such contacts played an important part in forming people's ideas about who they were and who other people were.

IDENTITY

The beginning of this chapter presents names that late Roman and other writers used to designate the peoples of Europe in the fifth through eighth centuries. I turn now to the question of how these peoples identified themselves. Because none of these societies became fully literate in the period we are considering, and thus there is no comprehensive written record of how they defined who they were or thought about themselves in relation to others, we need to rely on other sources of information. Two kinds of material evidence are especially useful here. One is ritual; the other is design or style.

The fifth-century writer Jordanes describes how material objects were used in the funerary ritual of the Hunnic king Attila (chapter 2), who died in the year 453.

> His body was placed in the midst of a plain and lay in state in a silken tent as a sight for men's admiration. The best horsemen of the entire tribe of the Huns rode around in circles . . . and told of his deeds in a funeral dirge. . . . They gave way in turn to the extremes of feeling and displayed funereal grief alternating with joy. Then in the secrecy of night they buried his body in the earth. They bound his coffins, the first with gold, the second with silver and the third with the strength of iron . . . iron because he subdued the nations, gold and silver because he received the honors of both empires. They also added the arms of foemen won in the fight, trappings of rare worth, sparkling with various gems, and ornaments of all sorts whereby princely state is maintained.

This account gives a good impression of how the people known as the Huns represented their identity through the ritual of their leader's funeral (just as the funerals of modern heads of state are used to express important themes about national identity).

To see how cultural identities were expressed by different peoples in Europe, we can contrast Jordanes's description of Attila's funerary ceremony with the archaeological findings of the grave of an Anglo-Saxon king (perhaps a king whose name was Raedwald, although it is not certain that he was the man buried in this grave) found at Sutton Hoo, in East Anglia in England. While horses played a major role in the ritual celebrating Attila, at Sutton Hoo the important vehicle was a boat, a wooden ship eighty-nine feet long buried in the ground and on which a burial chamber was constructed. The traditional symbols of the male leader in western Europe were included in the grave—sword, shield, battle-ax, and helmet. Dining equipment amounting to twenty-two vessels—ten silver bowls, a silver dish, two drinking horns, six wooden bottles with gilt silver bands of ornament, and three bronze cauldrons—underscore this ruler's role as host of feasts, similar to that of the king portrayed in the epic poem *Beowulf*, which recounts the mythic adventures of heroes from this time. The origins of the grave goods tell us something of the interregional connections of this early-seventh-century king. The ornate helmet was made in Scandinavia. The lavishly ornamented gold belt buckle and the sword with gold pommel and hilt were products of continental workshops. The thirty-seven coins found in a purse are from the Frankish region across the English Channel. The silver bowls and dish were made in the Byzantine east Mediterranean region, and the silver dish bears stamps of official workshops of the Byzantine emperor Anastasius I, who ruled from 491 to 518.

The new style of ornament represented on the belt buckle, the purse lid, and the weapons in the Sutton Hoo grave is another important indicator of the marking of new identities. This style is made up of three main elements. One is chip-carving, a technique that involved casting and then cutting chips out of a slab of bronze, silver, or gold to create numerous facets to catch the light. The second is cloisonné, the fitting of cut garnet (a brilliant red stone) into gold settings on the surface of personal ornaments, weapons, and metal vessels. The third is stylized representations of animals and humans with particular emphasis on heads and faces. The development of this new style in fifth- and sixth-century Europe parallels the emergence of new nations, including those of the Franks in the Rhineland and France, the Alamanni in southwest Germany, and the Anglo-Saxons in England. This style, referred to as animal ornament or Germanic art, marked the identity of members of these newly formed nations just as flags represent modern countries and specific insignia represent sports teams. Although the new style as a whole indicated the creation of a new consciousness on the part of peoples who felt themselves free of Roman domination, each region developed its own distinctive decorative details. An Anglo-Saxon brooch is recognizably different from a Frankish brooch, for example (see chapter 11).

The placement of objects decorated with the new styles is indicative of their importance as media of communication. All were prominently displayed—brooches worn on the front of a person's shoulder, pendants around the neck or fastened to the chest, sword handles at a warrior's side, and the often richly ornamented front surface of a shield held out for all to see.

By the end of our period, as the kingdoms of the Franks, the Anglo-Saxons, and the rest emerged as powerful new political entities in post-Roman Europe, there are signs that some rulers wished to draw connections between themselves and the Roman emperors of half a millennium earlier—in other words,

Figure 3.2. Drawing of a bronze belt buckle ornamented with the technique known as chip-carving, from Smithfield, London (length 3⅔ inches). The object was cast, with the decorative pattern carved into the stone mold. After casting, the surface was worked with a sharp iron burin or fine chisel to create the distinct pattern of ridges and grooves. This technique was important for the manufacture of many decorative objects during late Roman and post-Roman times.

to identify their rule with that of Rome as it was remembered through oral histories and the few surviving written documents. This desire is particularly evident in Charlemagne, the emergent king of the Franks from the late eighth century, who was crowned Emperor of the Romans by the Pope in Rome on Christmas Day in the year 800. Einhard, a member of Charlemagne's court, provides a description of Charlemagne's clothing and personal equipment that links him closely to the traditions mentioned in this chapter.

> He wore the national dress of the Franks . . . a linen shirt . . . [and] linen pants. Over these he put on a tunic trimmed at the border with silk. The legs from the knee downward were wound with leggings, fastened around the calves with laces, and on his feet he wore boots. In winter he protected his shoulders and chest with a vest made of otter skins or marten fur, and over that he wrapped a blue cloak. He always carried a sword strapped to his side, and the hilt and belt . . . were made . . . of gold or silver. . . . On high festival days he wore a suit of golden cloth and boots ornamented with jewels. His cloak was fastened with a golden brooch, and on his head he carried a diadem of gold, embellished with gems.

When Charlemagne built his imperial capital at Aachen, he created two separate but physically connected buildings to represent the linking of his political power with his religious authority. He constructed a hall in the northern part of the complex and a chapel in the southern part. The hall had its roots in the halls of earlier times, such as that at Gudme in Denmark (chapter 7), though his immediate inspiration seems to have been the hall built by the Roman emperor Constantine at Trier. The chapel was modeled on the church of San Vitale in Ravenna, constructed by the emperor Justinian. As if his crowning as Emperor of the Romans, in Rome, were not enough to make clear his identification with Roman glories, for the construction of his chapel he had stone removed from buildings in Rome and Ravenna, hauled north to Aachen, and integrated into the structure of his new church.

The person of Charlemagne thus links several important themes of this chapter and the book. His clothing, weaponry, and personal ornaments, and the architecture of his hall, emphasize his connection with his people, the Franks. The details of the design of his Royal Chapel, and the materials used to build it, as well as the circumstances of his crowning by the Pope in Rome, link him with the Roman emperors. And his construction of a monumental church, modeled on an important one in Italy, demonstrates his affiliation with the Christian Church.

Three centuries before Charlemagne, near the beginning of the Dark Ages, regional kings were rising to power in different parts of Europe. We know less about them historically than we do about Charlemagne, but we can learn a great deal from their graves. Whereas Charlemagne represents consolidated political power at the end of the Dark Ages, the men buried in graves discovered at Tournai in Belgium, Apahida in Romania, Blučina in the Czech Republic, Mezöberény in Hungary, Pouan in France, and Fürst in Germany represent the beginnings of the new societies that were emerging all across the continent of Europe as Roman power declined. The grave at Tournai, containing the remains of the Frankish king Childeric, is of special importance.

4
Childeric and Other Early Dark Age Kings

❖

WITH A QUICK AND WELL-AIMED SLASH, THE RAZOR-sharp short sword sliced through the neck of the sturdy stallion, and dark red blood spurted out, splashing the man and pouring onto the ground. The quivering horse sank to its knees with a jolt, then its hind legs collapsed. It fell slowly onto its right side and slid over the edge of the waiting pit, slumping to a position touching its master's coffin. During the next few minutes, fifty more horses died nearby in similar fashion, but the pits into which they fell were devoid of human occupants. The animals came to rest in pits that contained only the bodies of other horses, as many as seven in some, as few as four in others.

This sacrifice, this ritualized slaughter, of horses—the details of which I have imagined in the preceding paragraph—was part of the funerary celebration of Childeric, who was a king of the Franks and a loyal defender of what was left of the Roman Empire. The funeral, in the year A.D. 482, was a signal event in Europe's early history. Childeric embodied powers and signs of the now disintegrating Roman Empire at the same time that he symbolized the new themes of the emerging nations of medieval Europe. Childeric and his grave, which was discovered in 1653, can help us understand the relation between these two formative periods of European history.

NAPOLEON'S BEES

When Napoleon Bonaparte was crowned emperor of France on December 2, 1804, he had selected a symbol for his rule that would proclaim a new beginning for France and distinguish his dynasty from those of his Bourbon predecessors with their fleur-de-lis motif. Napoleon chose bees and had hundreds of small gold bees sewn onto his coronation mantle. Why bees?

Napoleon selected bees to create a link with Childeric, the father of Clovis, the first king of France. The grave of this Frankish king had contained hundreds of exquisite little gold bees inset with brilliant red garnets.

DISCOVERING CHILDERIC'S GRAVE

On May 27, 1653, a team of workmen was digging on a construction site just north of the church of St. Brice in Tournai, in Belgium. About eight feet below the surface, a laborer named Adrien Quinquin found a gold bracelet, and soon a great many small gold ornaments, gold and silver coins, pieces of iron, the skull of a horse, a crystal ball, fragments of human bone, and

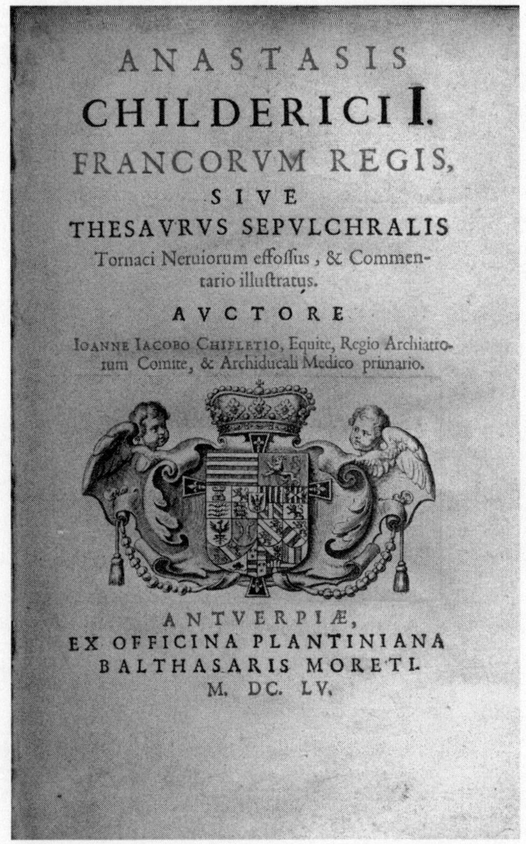

ANASTASIS
CHILDERICI I.
FRANCORVM REGIS,
SIVE
THESAVRVS SEPVLCHRALIS
Tornaci Neruiorum effoſſus, & Commentario illuſtratus.
AVCTORE
IOANNE IACOBO CHIFLETIO, Equite, Regio Archiatrorum Comite, & Archiducali Medico primario.

ANTVERPIÆ,
EX OFFICINA PLANTINIANA
BALTHASARIS MORETI.
M. DC. LV.

Figure 4.1. Title page of Chiflet's 1655 publication describing the Childeric grave, considered the first scientific archaeological publication in the world. This book, published in Antwerp (now in Belgium), was written in Latin, with Chiflet's name in Latinized form.

many other objects were uncovered. Among the treasures were hundreds of small bees made of gold inlaid with garnet.

The collection of objects that emerged from this building site was brought to the attention of Leopold Wilhelm, a Habsburg

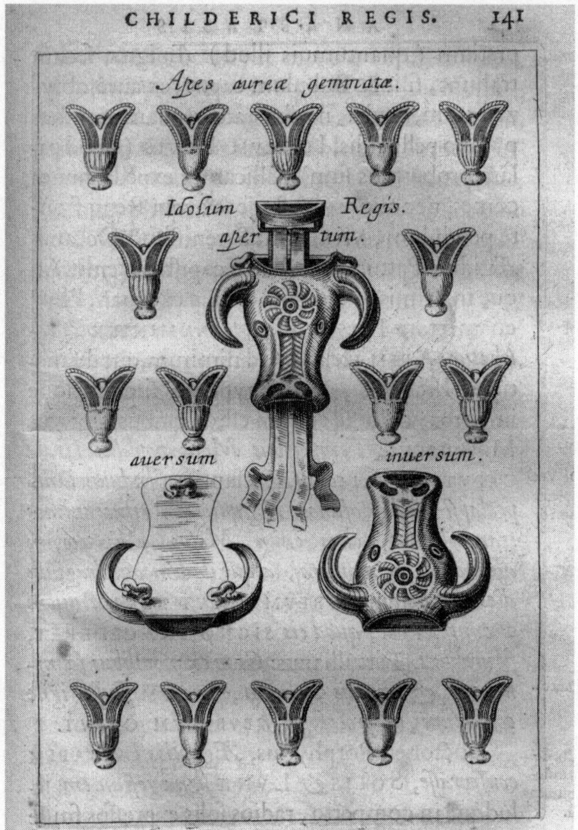

Figure 4.2. Drawing from Chiflet's publication of some of the gold-and-garnet bees and of the gold bull's head from Childeric's grave. The bees are about three-quarters of an inch long.

archduke who was serving as governor of what was then the Austrian Netherlands. Subsequent searching of the excavation site and gathering together of objects that had already been dispersed resulted in the accumulation of a substantial proportion of the items that had been in the grave. The archduke turned over the finds to Jean-Jacques Chiflet, his personal doctor. Besides practicing medicine, Chiflet (the name was sometimes spelled Chifflet) was a member of a learned family and an accomplished scholar himself. Three years earlier, in 1650, he had published a 328-page history of his home city of Besançon, in eastern France. That volume included maps, architectural drawings, and engravings of historical objects such as ceramic vessels and statues, attesting to Chiflet's qualifications to undertake the study and publication of this new find.

In 1655, two years after the discovery, Chiflet published his report on the objects that had been made available to him in a well-illustrated volume that is regarded as the world's first scientific archaeological publication. The title of the book, written—like most scientific works of the seventeenth century—in Latin, is *Anastasis Childerici I. Francorvm Regis, sive Thesavrvs Sepvlchralis Tornaci* (The Resurrection of Childeric the First, King of the Franks, or The Funerary Treasure of Tournai).

The later history of the extraordinary objects from the grave is less happy than we might hope from the auspicious early treatment of the finds. In 1656 the objects were brought from Brussels to the treasury in Vienna. Nine years later, in 1665, they were presented to King Louis XIV in Paris, where they were housed in the Royal Library until 1831. That year the majority of them were stolen. Only a handful of the objects survives today, including two of the gold and garnet bees. Fortunately, it has been possible for archaeologists to reconstruct the appearance of most of the objects from the grave on the basis of the excellent illustrations in Chiflet's publication, casts made of many of them before 1831, and copies made of some before the theft.

Among the numerous objects that were recovered from the grave, of unique importance is the gold signet ring. On the seal is a bust of a long-haired man wearing body armor and holding a spear in his right hand. Around his head is the Latin inscription CHILDERICI REGIS—of Childeric the King.

THE HISTORICAL CHILDERIC

Childeric, who lived from about 436 to 482, was arguably the first major king of post-Roman Europe. In the same way that Napoleon traced his claim to the kingship of France through Childeric, many other European rulers viewed Childeric as their political progenitor. He was the model for all later European kings.

The little we know about Childeric from surviving written sources can be summarized in two paragraphs. By the year 463, Childeric had become a man of significant military and political power, and from that year until 470 he is mentioned in several texts. He was a Frankish king, leader of the group known as Salian Franks in the north of Gaul (today northern France, Belgium, and the Netherlands and Germany west of the Rhine River). He commanded Frankish troops who helped defend what was left of the Roman Empire in that part of Europe. According to one account, he was the governor of the province Belgica Secunda, in northwestern Gaul. The written sources, scanty as they are, indicate that Childeric was a loyal ally of the late Roman emperors. He served with a Roman official named Aegidius in a major battle against an army of Visigoths, and he fought against Saxon pirates near the coastal town of Angers.

Childeric was the father of Clovis, who was only about sixteen years old when Childeric died. As king, Clovis greatly expanded the territorial domain of his people, the Franks. He was the first Frankish king to be baptized a Christian. Clovis is generally regarded as the founder of the Merovingian dynasty of early medieval Europe. Many historians consider the baptism of Clovis in 496 as the event that signified the emergence of France as a nation. Childeric, as Clovis's father, thus occupied a fundamental position in the political and cultural dynamics of early European society.

CHILDERIC'S FUNERAL

No description survives of Childeric's funeral and burial. But let us imagine what it must have been like based on the rich assemblage of objects in his grave and what we know about royal funerals in early Europe.

A large crowd—nearly a thousand people—had gathered at dawn to witness the funeral spectacle. The death of a king was an important event because it left a chasm in the social order. Who would fill it? An obvious successor, such as Childeric's sixteen-year-old son, Clovis? Or would rivals contest the succession and fight for their own elevation to kingship? The mood was tense because no one knew who would emerge from the ceremony as the designated successor.

The assembled group was diverse, with many different stations in life represented by people who had come to bid their king farewell and learn who would succeed him. The group included warrior followers of Childeric who had served him courageously in battle. Most of them would fight to ensure Clovis's place in the succession. But a few wavered in their loyalty, feeling that Childeric had not rewarded them adequately for their faithful service. The crowd also included village elders from tens of miles around representing their communities at this important political occasion. Local peasant farmers also attended, their main interest being to honor the ruler who had provided them with two decades of prosperity in what might have been a tumultuous time for them. And they were intensely curious to learn who their next king would be.

All waited in anticipation of the performance of the funerary ritual, wondering whether Childeric's close counselors would be able to orchestrate the ceremony in such a way that Clovis emerged from the event as the only reasonable successor to his father's authority. Although the occasion was solemn, an animated murmur could be heard throughout the crowd as people speculated about what was to unfold before them. The only other sounds were the neighing of horses coming from behind them and the occasional cawing of a crow overhead.

For the king's immediate counselors, who had planned and would orchestrate the event, the critical goal was to instill in the memories of all participants—advisers, warriors, and common people—the symbols and meanings of this extraordinary event. They would use sights, sounds, and smells to create a performance that would forever be fresh in the memories of participants and witnesses alike. In the process of the ritual, they would see to it that Childeric's power was transferred smoothly and without interruption to the sixteen-year-old boy. They had everything carefully planned. They had prepared their king's body with the most important of his personal decorations arranged in highly visible locations, and they would make full use of the significance of each object to those at the ceremony who understood them, and at the same time impress those who did not fully understand the meaning of all the objects they would see pass before their eyes. They would introduce, in highly visible fashion and with attendant speeches, other objects that conveyed the meanings that were important for their purposes—the ornate weapons as symbols of Childeric's status as a war leader, the gold coins as signs of the Byzantine emperor's esteem for the Frankish king, and the gold crossbow brooch that attested to his favor among the late Roman potentates. Still, they felt tense at the beginning of the ceremony. Although they had planned everything in great detail, something could still go wrong.

The crowd heard the low tones of a dirge coming from their right, to the south of the open burial pit. It was sung by a hundred warriors decked out in their military garments, their swords hanging at their sides. Six at the front bore on their shoulders the plain wooden coffin of their king. As they stepped slowly forward in the direction of the waiting grave, many in the crowd joined the singing of the funeral melody, and the sound grew louder in the morning air. The advancing procession, the rising strains of the dirge, and the smell of the horses created a powerful atmosphere of strangeness, of a world very different from the everyday. A few feet from the grave, the bearers lowered the coffin and set it on the ground. One man slowly and gently lifted the plank lid and set it aside, exposing the dead king to the view of everyone nearby.

Those in the front of the crowd moved forward to see their king. He lay outfitted in his finest tunic, belt, stockings, and leather boots. His woolen cloak, which was parted to expose the ornaments on his chest, had attached to it hundreds of small gold bees with inlaid garnets, the metal and the stone sparkling in the morning sun. His golden belt buckle and shoe buckles also shone in the sun, but the most striking sights were three other objects crafted from gold. They had been arranged to be clearly visible to the officials and warriors in the front rows of spectators.

One was the gold signet ring, set on the ring finger of his right hand, which had been placed on his stomach. This solid gold ring, which bore the image of the king, showed him as a Roman military leader, with a coat of body armor, and also as a Germanic king, with long hair and spear. Around the image was the inscription CHILDERICI REGIS, a Germanic name written in Latin and Roman script. The observers in the front knew that this ring symbolized Childeric's complex role as a Germanic king and as a defender of the Roman Empire.

The second object was a solid gold bracelet that the dead king wore on his right wrist. This showed that Childeric belonged to a group of powerful kings whose domains included most of early medieval Europe.

The third object was the gold onion-head fibula. This brooch had been presented to Childeric by Roman officials to acknowledge his services to the late empire.

The messages implicit in these objects were fully understood by the local chiefs and warriors in the front of the throng. Among those of lesser status—the peasants and crafts workers—only a few caught distant glimpses of the gleaming gold and sparkling garnet. Although not appreciating the specific associations of each of these ornaments, they understood that the objects reflected the wider importance of their dead king.

The ceremony took a new direction. A man stepped forward toward the coffin. He held in his outstretched hands Childeric's ceremonial sword, its hilt decorated with gold and garnet, its scabbard a veritable band of gleaming metal and flashing red stone. The sword was the symbol par excellence of elite male status in European society. Of all the powerful symbols displayed during the funeral ceremony, of all the gold objects that told of Childeric's status in one domain or the other, nothing was as potently evocative of his status and power as the gold-encrusted sword. After holding the sword high for all the assembled crowd to see and evoking the approval of the gods (there is no evidence to suggest that Childeric was Christian), the man slowly and deliberately placed the sword in the coffin on Childeric's left side. He continued with the warrior-king's lesser weapons—the short sword, lance, ax—saying with each a few words about Childeric's valor, loyalty to his people, and exemplary qualities of leadership.

Childeric's prized steed was brought forward. Neighing furiously and resisting the tugs of the grooms, the horse was led to the edge of the grave pit. The man near the coffin raised his arms toward the sky, again invoking the attention of the gods, then turned quickly and slashed open the restrained horse's throat. Blood gushed onto the freshly piled soil. The horse staggered, collapsed onto its front knees, rolled sideways, and fell into the grave.

From the side, a procession of fifty warriors emerged on horseback, all members of Childeric's elite companions in combat. They rode around the grave and its surrounding mound, circling in a clockwise direction, all the time singing praises of their fallen leader. Clovis stepped forward with a shovel. He thrust the blade into the dirt piled next to the grave pit and gently tossed the shovelful of fresh earth onto his father's coffin. Twenty men stepped up to join him. As they worked, the center of the mound rose ever higher, finally forming a dome of earth some sixty-five feet in diameter and six feet high over the grave.

When the piling of earth onto the mound was finished, the riding warriors slowed their pace, then guided their steeds toward one of eight open pits that lay at the edge of the mound. One at a time, each warrior approached the edge of a pit, dismounted, and slashed the throat of his horse, allowing it to fall bleeding into the pit, as had been done with Childeric's horse earlier. Altogether, fifty horses were killed and buried at short distances from the mound that covered the king's grave.

Finally, as befit every king, his followers announced that the funerary feast was ready. The mourners turned their attention from the newly heaped mound and slowly walked a short distance toward the west, away from the mound and the horse graves, to a spot where meat was roasting on spits and beer was waiting in great ceramic jugs. Childeric's bards continued to sing his praises as the party settled onto rude wooden benches to begin the feast.

Thus ends our imaginary vision of Childeric's funeral. What does the archaeology of his grave tell us?

ARCHAEOLOGY OF CHILDERIC'S GRAVE

Childeric's grave is the richest burial known from the Merovingian period (A.D. 450–751) in Europe. Unlike many of the well-outfitted burials of the time, it had not been looted by tomb robbers. But because it was discovered so long ago, before the development of scientific techniques of excavation and recording, there is no information about the arrangement of objects in the tomb. But the contents reveal a great deal about this man and the role that he, and other kings of comparable status, played in the waning years of Roman power.

Unique is Childeric's finger ring, with his portrait and his name and title in Latin. This object is the most important in identifying the grave as that of Childeric, and the image represents the man with respect to his complex identity in the Roman and Germanic worlds of the late fifth century. The idea of the portrait is Roman, as is the character of the armor he is shown wearing. But his long hair and the lance in his right hand are signs of Germanic kingship.

The weapons indicate that he was buried as a military leader

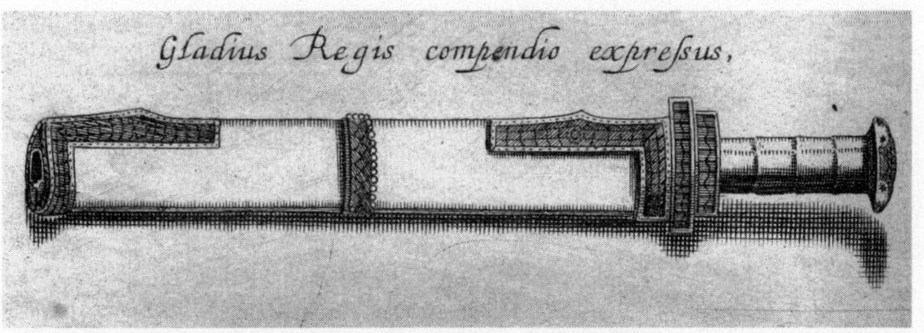

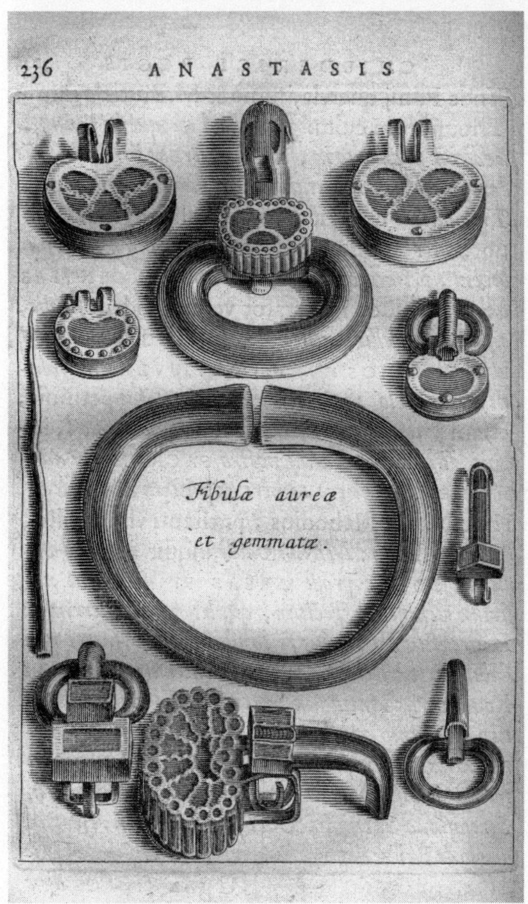

Figure 4.3. *Above*, drawing from Chiflet's publication of the sword in its scabbard (length about 16 inches) from Childeric's grave. The pommel at the end of the grip is gold and in the form of two birds' heads. The grip is coated with sheet gold. The guard and the trim on the scabbard are of gold inset with garnet.

Figure 4.4. *Left*, the gold bracelet (center) and gold buckles, most of them inset with garnet, from the Childeric grave. The maximum width of the bracelet is about 3 inches.

of high distinction. He had the full component of weapons of his day—a long sword, a short sword, a lance, and a throwing ax. A fragment of iron that Chiflet thought belonged to a horseshoe may have been part of a grip from a shield. Two of Childeric's weapons were different from those buried in the majority of warriors' graves. The hilt of the long sword was made of bone and covered with gold, and the pommel and guards were of gold inset with cut garnets. The pommel was further ornamented with two bird heads, the shape of their beaks indicating that they were birds of prey. The scabbards of the long and short swords were also decorated with gold inset with garnets and included ornaments in the form of bird heads.

Childeric's personal ornaments of gold, also often inlaid with cut garnets, indicate that he was a person of high status in his society. The pattern of ornament on two large buckles made of gold with inset garnets matches the gold and garnet decoration on the scabbards for the long and short swords. These buckles probably were parts of belts from which the swords were suspended. Though no textile remains were reported from the grave, Chiflet mentions gold threads, which were commonly woven into fabrics worn by elites. The solid gold bracelet is similar to those found in eight other graves of this period, all of them richly outfitted. The bracelets are thought to have been worn by Germanic kings during the second half of the fifth century as a sign of their authority. Two attachments for a leather purse were made in the shape of horses, with garnets inset in the gold. This was probably the purse that Chiflet said was found in the lap of Childeric's remains. Chiflet reported more than three hundred gold-and-garnet bees found in the grave. Aegidius Patte, the priest of St. Brice, where the grave was found, asserted that the bees were part of decorations associated with the skeletal remains of the horse mentioned in connection with the find, and Chiflet reports this account. But many subsequent investigators believe that this is wrong and that the bees were sewn (using little loops on the backs of the bees) onto a cloak that Childeric wore. Representations of bees in association with horses have been found at sites of the fourth and fifth centuries in lands along the middle and lower Danube in eastern Europe. Also reported as associated with the horse skeleton in Childeric's grave was a gold bull's head, which had been hollow cast and the features of which—eyes, ears, horns, and a spiral disk on the forehead—were inset with garnets.

Other objects in the grave tell important things about Childeric's role in the wider world beyond northeastern Gaul. The gold fibula is of special significance. Brooches of this kind were presented by late Roman emperors and other high officials to individuals of high rank in return for special service to the Empire. Similar fibulae have been found in other rich warrior burials in other parts of Europe (see below). The representation of Childeric on his signet ring shows him wearing such a fibula.

Chiflet informs us that a leather purse containing more than a hundred gold coins and two hundred of silver lay in the lap area of the skeleton. The gold coins, Roman solidi, are almost all types minted during the second half of the fifth century in Constantinople under the auspices of the emperors of the eastern Roman Empire. The earliest were minted during the reign of Theodosius II in the middle of the fifth century, the latest under the emperor Zeno, who ruled from 476 to 491. They probably represent a payment made by Zeno to Childeric for his services as a military protector of the Empire's interests in northern Gaul.

Of the two hundred silver coins that Chiflet reports, he was able to secure only forty-two for his work on the publication. The silver coins are different in character and significance from the gold coins. The earliest silver coin was minted during the Roman Republic (pre-27 B.C.), and many different periods, all before A.D. 480, are represented. Four had been perforated for stringing on a necklace or bracelet or wearing as pendants.

MODERN EXCAVATIONS IN THE CEMETERY

Between 1983 and 1986, Raymond Brulet conducted archaeological excavations near where the Childeric grave had been found three centuries earlier. Because the area is within the city of Tournai, and because Chiflet did not provide a map showing where the grave was situated, its exact location is uncertain. In his excavations, Brulet uncovered ninety-three graves dating from the middle of the fifth to the early part of the seventh century. He identified within the cemetery an open space about 65 feet in diameter where there were no graves. Brulet interprets this open area as the site where a mound once stood over Childeric's grave. On the outer edge of this open area, Brulet found the three large pits containing the complete skeletons of twenty-one horses, as described in the reconstruction above. Marks on some of the skeletons indicate that the animals were killed with slashes to the neck.

MEANING OF THE GRAVE

Childeric's grave was situated about 650 feet from the late Roman fort of Tornacum, an indication of a link between the king and the symbol of imperial power in the region. The objects show how the different roles that Childeric played were represented through material culture. In this one find, all of the major strains in the cultural dynamics of the fifth and sixth centuries are evident.

Similarities between the materials in Childeric's grave and those in a series of other richly outfitted graves of the period link this group in important ways. These links played critical roles in the creation of the new societies that developed during the sixth, seventh, and eighth centuries and led to the emergence of the historical kingdoms of the Middle Ages and thence to the modern nations of Europe.

A brief look at five of these other graves from the second half of the fifth century highlights the connections between these ruling elites in the different regions.

APAHIDA II

An understanding of Childeric's grave, and its wider significance in Europe, is richly enhanced by the discovery of a grave that bears important similarities to it, eight hundred miles to the southeast, at Apahida in Transylvania, Romania. The fact that a strikingly similar burial should be found such a distance away underscores the pan-European nature of these remains.

Like the Childeric grave, the Apahida II burial was found in the course of construction work, in this case digging to build the foundation for a cement pole to hold streetlights. The discovery was made in October 1968. The two workmen who found the material divided the gold objects between them and sold about three ounces of gold, which was subsequently worked into jewelry. When the local archaeological authorities learned about the find four months later, most of the objects were still intact and could be acquired by the historical museum in Cluj, a city just west of Apahida.

Excavations carried out in May 1969 revealed the burial pit, remains of a wooden coffin, and horse harness gear. Part of the grave had been destroyed by the earlier digging. The parts of the skeleton that survived indicate that the man had been exceptionally large—about six feet three inches tall—and had been buried on his back with his head in the western end of the grave. The systematic excavation of the intact portion of the grave enabled the archaeologists to pinpoint the locations of grave goods with respect to the skeleton and one another, important for understanding the purposes of the objects. An iron long sword was situated on the right side of the man. Ornaments associated with his belt were found around his knees, perhaps because when the lid of the coffin collapsed as the wood rotted, it pushed the decaying leather belt from his waist to this lower part of his body. Near his feet were three iron bits for horses and attachments for a saddle. Nearby was a gold-plated iron socket. A glass beaker was found outside the coffin.

Like the Childeric grave, iron weapons formed an important part of the burial assemblage in Apahida II. A long sword, a socket that was probably for a lance head, and a knife were made of iron. The sword scabbard was ornamented with gold and inset garnets, the knife had a handle of sheet gold, and a buckle that was probably part of the weapon-bearing belt was made of gold with inset garnets. Other buckles and strap ends of gold and garnet may have been attached to the weapon belt, or they may have been parts of his personal outfit.

Objects of personal ornament included gold-and-garnet shoe buckles, strap ends, and gold beads. A large purse with a gold-and-garnet lid in elaborate patterning, and the remains of a smaller purse, were parts of the individual's personal equipment.

Associated with horseback riding are numerous ornaments of gold and garnet. These include two striking figures of eagles four inches high thought to be part of the saddle decoration.

About five hundred yards west of Apahida II, a richly outfitted burial had been found in 1889, also dating to the second half of the fifth century and also having strong similarities to the Childeric find. Apahida I contained an onion-head fibula of gold, a gold arm ring with thickened ends, and a gold ring bearing the name of this burial individual—Omharus. Unlike Childeric, Omharus is not mentioned in any known written source.

BLUČINA

Near Brno, in the Czech Republic, a richly outfitted grave of a man between thirty and forty years of age was discovered at Blučina and excavated in 1953. Like the Childeric and Apahida II graves, this one contained a long sword and a short sword, both decorated with gold and garnets, and a gold bracelet with thickened ends, as well as numerous other ornaments of gold, garnet, and silver. In this carefully excavated grave, the long sword was on the man's left side and the short sword and bow on his right. Next to his lower right leg was a wooden saddle with silver ornaments along its edges. Three glass vessels had been arranged at his feet, along with a comb carved from bone with rivets inlaid with garnets.

Personal ornaments besides the gold bracelet included a silver fibula, an iron belt buckle with a gold-and-garnet ornament, and a gilded silver attachment at the end of a leather belt. His shoes were decorated with gold-and-garnet buckles and rings, similar to objects found in Childeric's grave. Hence Childeric was probably buried wearing shoes much like those in the Blučina grave.

In this grave, the saddle and the bow are objects characteristic of areas farther to the east among peoples for whom horseback riding was a vital cultural practice. The long and short swords and the buckles are especially characteristic of western regions.

POUAN

A grave found by workmen in 1842 in Pouan, in northeastern France, contained, like Childeric's tomb and Apahida II, ornate long and short swords, a gold bracelet with thickened ends, and a gold finger ring with an inscribed name—HEVA. As in the case of Apahida, no written sources tell who this person was. Two gold buckles with cloisonné garnet inlay and two solid gold buckles are among other objects recovered from this burial.

FÜRST

A grave discovered in 1843 in southern Germany contained the skeleton of a young man. Reported from this burial are a gold bracelet similar in form to those in the other graves discussed above, three solid gold buckles with garnet inlay, and a beaker made of green glass. Other objects that were recovered have been lost. From the few documented items, it is apparent that the person buried here shared at least some of the special status represented by the gold objects in these special graves.

MEZÖBERÉNY

In 1884, a grave was found near Békés, Hungary, but again a full report of its character is lacking. A gold bracelet similar in form to those in the Childeric, Apahida, and Blučina graves was recovered, indicating a link to them. No weapons were reported from this find, but many ornaments of gold inlaid with garnets were discovered. They included a small insect, a pair of earrings, a pair of buckles, two strap ends, and four sheet gold attachments, perhaps for some kind of head ornament. The gold-and-garnet jewelry links this find with the burials discussed above and suggests a similar degree of wealth and status. The small sizes of the ornaments, and the lack of any trace of weapons, has led to the suggestion that these objects may have been buried with a young girl, perhaps the daughter of a ruler of the status of Childeric in western Europe and of the man buried at Apahida II in the east.

RULERS OF EARLY POST-ROMAN EUROPE

Of the series of richly outfitted, apparently royal, burials of the second half of the fifth century, only for Childeric is there textual information to broaden our understanding of the significance of the objects included in the grave. But the striking similarity between the Childeric grave and the others shows that individuals of status comparable to Childeric lived in different parts of Europe and were part of a shared system of symbols and meanings. The special objects included gold bracelets, gold fibulae, gold-and-garnet ornament on weapons and garments, sets of iron weapons, and horse-related items, which could be actual horses, trappings, or stylistic representations of horses' heads. But regional distinctions between these burial assemblages are also significant. Childeric, in the northwestern ("Frankish") part of the continent, shows a stronger representation of weaponry than do comparable graves in central and eastern Europe. In the eastern burials, objects associated with horses—saddles and decorations on harnesses—play a major role in the rich graves. In the east, the eagle motif, which later becomes a principal motif in the arts and decorations of the early medieval period, is abundantly represented on the large and highly ornate purse lid, the sword scabbard, and the ornamental buttons of Apahida II. Birds of prey—perhaps eagles—are also represented in the Childeric grave on the pommels of the swords, but in less striking fashion than at Apahida.

Using traditional signs, if we consider Childeric's gold onion-head fibula, his signet ring with the Latin inscription, his portrayal on the ring wearing the armor of a Roman officer, and his coins, we could argue that Childeric was "Roman"—that he identified himself with the Roman Empire. But if we focus instead on his weapon set, his other gold jewelry, and all of the horse-riding accoutrements, we could identify Childeric as a typical elite male in the European tradition from the Bronze Age on. If instead of either the Roman or the traditional materials we focus on new elements in the grave that bespeak neither a Roman affiliation nor a link with local traditions—the gold-and-garnet ornaments, the bees, the bull's head, the crystal ball—we see that he, as a person, and the funerary ceremony that honored his death represent something new on the scene of late fifth-century Europe.

Childeric's grave, and others that share much of the symbolism of Germanic royalty and Roman alliance, is a perfect representation of the changes that were taking place in the latter half of the fifth century in Europe. The idea of Rome and its empire was still very much alive in the minds of the rulers, and they decorated themselves with signs of their connection to that power. But new ideals and new political structures were gaining momentum, and Childeric's grave reflects these new themes in abundance. The importance of Childeric and his grave for the later history of Europe is evident in Charlemagne's drawing directly on the historical tradition of that first Frankish king who ruled three centuries before he did, and in Napoleon's efforts, another thousand years later, to adopt symbols from Childeric's grave to further his own political ends.

While Childeric's grave informs us about the nature of royalty and its symbolism in the first century of the Dark Ages, the fate of the Roman cities reveals the character of the urban populations after the Empire declined.

5
What Happened to the Roman Cities?

❖

THE MASSIVE STONE WALLS OF THE ROMAN FORTRESS at Regensburg are an integral and living part of today's cityscape. Regensburg, with a population of 130,000, is situated at the northernmost reach of the Danube River on its 1,800-mile course eastward to the Black Sea. The place was the site of a major military base and civilian town during the Roman period, and it emerged as an important church and commercial center throughout the Middle Ages. The wall around the largest of three Roman forts at Regensburg, built on the south bank of the river, was constructed of enormous blocks of limestone and sandstone, some as large as a cubic meter. The fort, built just above the flood level of the Danube, measured 1,620 by 1,350 feet. The survival of extensive sections of the Roman walls gives the city an extraordinary feel, as though the past never left. Major buildings—some medieval,

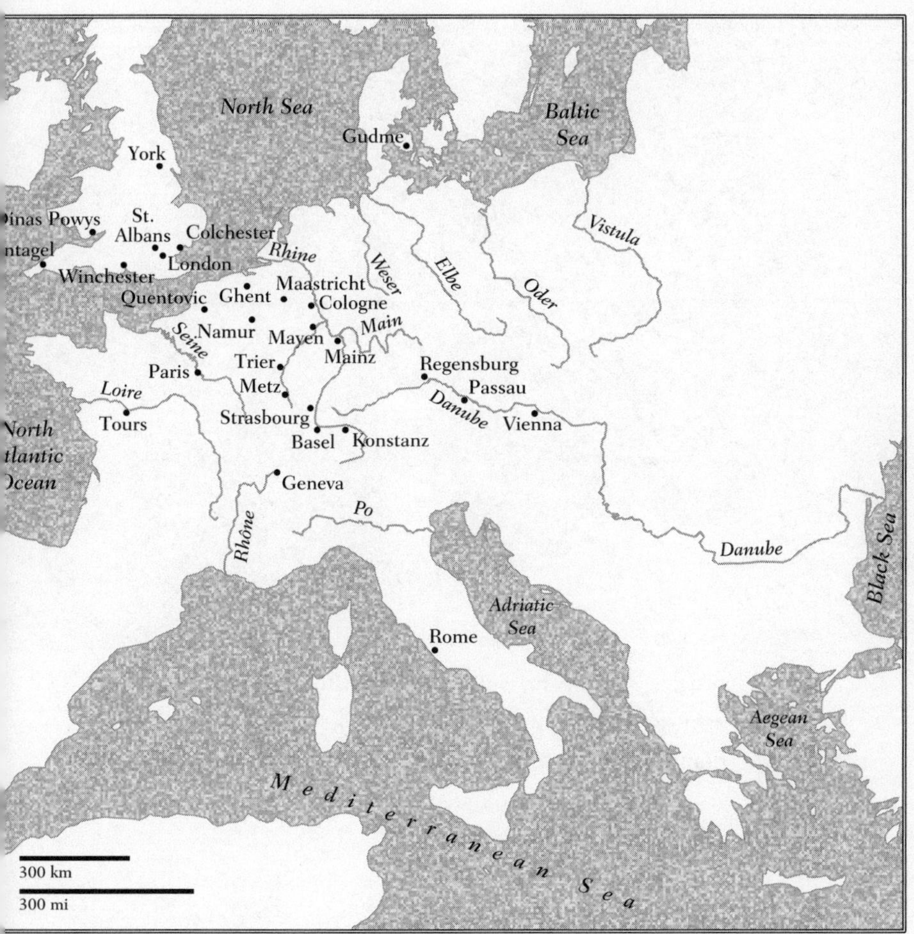

Figure 5.1. Places mentioned in chapters 5 and 6.

some modern—in the central part of the city employ the massive stone blocks of the Roman wall as important parts of their foundations.

To judge by these extensive walls, the Roman town survived into the Dark Ages, through the High Middle Ages, and into the twenty-first century. Was this characteristic of Roman cities?

Figure 5.2. Part of the wall around the Roman fortress at Regensburg, built of unusually large blocks of cut stone. The Roman wall still forms the foundation for buildings in the modern city.

CITIES, CIVILIZATION, AND THE QUESTION OF DECLINE

At the peak of the Roman Empire's power and wealth during the first and second centuries, about 15 percent of its total population lived in cities and towns. Italy and the provinces around the eastern shores of the Mediterranean had many more substantial towns than did the imperial regions of temperate Europe. Along the Rhine, the Danube, and the Thames, even the largest towns, such as Cologne, Mainz, Regensburg, and London, probably had populations of no more than 20,000 people at the most. The majority of people in the European provinces north of the Alps lived on farms or in small villages. Numbers recently suggested for Roman Britain are around four million people total, with about a quarter of a million in towns and cities, an eighth of a million in the military, and about three and a half million in rural areas.

Traditionally, historians have believed that towns and cities in Roman Europe declined during the fourth and fifth centuries, with the result that the succeeding populations were much more rural than they had been at the height of the Empire. But recent archaeological investigations show that this was not the case everywhere and may have been the exception rather than the rule.

ROME

In Rome itself, during the late Roman period and the Dark Ages, there was a shift from a political capital to a center of a rapidly expanding religious empire, with no indication of decline in population or overall activity.

As the result of military and political events during the third century, from the latter part of that century on, Rome was no longer the capital of the Empire (chapter 2). It remained the "spiritual" capital, but the practical functioning of the imperial government, along with the emperors' residences, shifted northward. Rome remained the center of the Christian Church, and hence its religious function continued to be important. Examining the character and economic activity of Rome during these later periods of the Empire is difficult, because archaeologists have concentrated on the period of Rome's greatest power and prosperity, during the first and second centuries, and have devoted somewhat less attention to the later deposits.

There is no reason to think that the population of Rome declined after the city lost its role as political capital to Milan, in the north. Its people probably still numbered around a million. Some texts from the sixth century mention the dismantling of buildings for their stone blocks, and some of the limestone from such buildings seems to have ended up in lime kilns. Yet despite Rome's loss of its political importance as capital of the Empire and all of the problems associated with the arrival of invading armies in the fifth century, the building of large and ornate churches from the fifth century on attests to the city's continuing religious, cultural, and economic significance. What some local writers considered to be decline of the former grand imperial capital others viewed as its transformation. Rome's central and dominant role in the rapidly growing Christian Church was paramount, and the city increasingly became a magnet for pilgrims.

REGENSBURG

Regensburg shows the transformation of a major military base and civilian settlement of the later Roman period to a political, religious, and economic center of the early Middle Ages.

The Roman bases at Regensburg were established there to guard the northernmost part of the Danube frontier of the Empire, and the civilian settlement grew up around the substantial military population. With the disintegration of Roman power in the fifth century, a major military presence there was no longer tenable. Many modern researchers have thought that the city was abandoned, perhaps overrun by peoples crossing the Danube to settle in the formerly Roman provincial lands.

But Regensburg contains good evidence for what happened to the city and the urban population during the fifth through eighth centuries. In recent decades, archaeologists have uncovered considerable evidence of continuing activity there. In much of the city, Roman period occupation layers are well preserved, as are layers representing early medieval activity. In the course of the fourth century, the character of Regensburg

Figure 5.3. The Roman fortress wall at Regensburg, just beyond the two bicyclists, showing how the two-thousand-year-old structure is integrated into the modern cityscape.

Figure 5.4. The structures built of large stone blocks are remains of the north gate to the Roman fort at Regensburg. This gate faced the Danube River, now just a hundred yards to the left of this view.

gradually changed. The size of the legionary contingent in the base was reduced to about a thousand men from the earlier five thousand or so, and the city took on a more civilian character. Although textual sources dealing with changes in the early fifth century indicate that the Third Italian Legion was moved out of Regensburg altogether after more than two centuries of being based in the fortress, there is no archaeological evidence for destruction or even rapid abandonment of the site. No massive burned layers have been identified, or crumbled ruins of Roman walls buried beneath later urban structures. Instead, people continued to live in Regensburg, and there is nothing to suggest a population decline, let alone abandonment. Even the name of the place was maintained—from Roman Castra Regina to medieval Reganespurc to modern German Regensburg.

Excavations beneath the Niedermünster church, near the center of the Roman and the modern city, revealed layers of sediment containing pottery made during the fifth century. Some showed strong continuity with provincial Roman traditions of ceramics, some of which were handmade and similar to the late prehistoric Iron Age wares of the area. An example of this hybridizing of craft traditions in pottery is a large jar that embodies elements of provincial Roman and indigenous traditions. Its shape and incised ornament are characteristic of local pottery, but it is glazed and has a high, thin handle—features of the provincial Roman tradition. Similar deposits of this period have been identified elsewhere in Regensburg. In some places, a thick layer of "dark earth" has been identified, much like that in London during the same period (chapter 6). Like the London layer, it indicates the changed use of the urban landscape but active occupation. A late-eighth-century text that mentions the Roman walls at Regensburg makes clear that they were still intact and served as defining and protective structures for the city's population.

MAINZ

At Mainz, there is unique evidence of the practice of pre-Christian religious rituals in the context of the Roman city, unusual remains of the destruction of a late Roman Rhine River fleet early in the Dark Ages, and the continuity of the settlement as a major early medieval trade port on the middle Rhine.

Like Regensburg, Mainz was established first as a Roman military base, but a couple of generations earlier. Mainz, at the confluence of the Main River into the Rhine, was founded around 12 B.C. with the building of a legionary base high above the Rhine on the west bank, just opposite the mouth of the Main. Today, standing at the front of the citadel constructed on this same spot in the late seventeenth cen-

Figure 5.5. Rhine River at Mainz, Germany. This view looks north from the west bank of the river (where Mainz is situated) toward the Taunus hills in the background. The Main River flows into the Rhine one and one-quarter miles upstream from this point (to the right), forming an important confluence at Mainz. Both banks here are low, affording easy crossing even with simple boats.

tury, one has a full panoramic view across the modern city of Mainz to the Rhine, about six hundred yards away, and across the broad flat plains on the other side. To the left, in the distance, are the Taunus hills; to the right, the confluence of the Main, flowing westward from the central regions of Germany into the Rhine. Early in the first century, the Roman base at Mainz was intended to serve as a staging site for Roman incursions eastward across the Rhine into Germanic territory. Roman Mainz became the capital of the province of Germania superior.

Recent excavations in the center of modern Mainz have revealed a religious site that tells much about the cult practices of the inhabitants of Roman cities. The findings provide a good picture of some of the pre-Christian ritual activity characteristic of Roman Europe. In the course of construction work for a new downtown shopping mall, archaeologists uncovered stone foundations of a major religious complex dedicated to the worship of the goddesses Isis and Mater Magna. This sanctuary was established during the first century, and it remained in use until the end of the third century, when much changed for Mainz and the Roman world as a whole. Unusual about these discoveries in Mainz was the extraordinary preservation of numerous small deposits of offerings and remains of fireplaces where offerings were burned, providing a very detailed view into ritual practices that preceded the introduction of Christianity in the fourth century.

The Roman sanctuary was constructed on what was already sacred ground to the local inhabitants of the region, marked by prehistoric burial mounds. In its first phase, the sanctuary comprised several small, rectangular temple buildings, but during the second century a larger, multi-room structure was built. Foundations were of stone and cement; the walls were of timber and plaster, painted with bright colors and with pictures of deities.

In front of the structure were fireplaces where people brought and burned their offerings to the gods. These included local foods, such as cereal grains, nuts, and fruit, and imported foods, including figs, dates, olives, and wine grapes. More than 90 percent of the animal bones recovered were those of chickens; most of the rest were of songbirds. Lamps made of pottery and fueled with olive oil were deposited in large numbers, perhaps one each time a person made an offering. Occasionally cattle skulls and even entire dogs were also offered. Sometimes small clay figurines of animals were offered instead of real animals. Other offerings included two clay dolls and a substantial number of lead tablets.

Such tablets, well known from many Roman period sites, are of special interest. They bear inscriptions revealing why they were deposited. These tablets were magical devices that people used as a means of asking favors from gods and spirits to exact revenge on other people, win the love of a desired person, or influence others in some other way. They show that, along with practicing the official Roman religions, people were also privately engaging in magic. The inscribed wish was incised with a stylus (a pointed iron implement in the shape of a pencil but thinner), perhaps by a professional scribe on behalf of the person desiring to cast a magic spell. Then the tablet was rolled into a cylinder or folded and deposited in the ground or in water.

After the disruptions of the third century, Mainz remained a significant Roman base and civilian settlement. Following its pullback from the *limes* boundary to the upper Rhine and upper Danube borders in the 260s, Rome began efforts to reconstitute its forces on the middle and upper Rhine to meet new defensive needs. Emphasis was shifted from large legionary units of troops stationed at major legionary bases to smaller units of troops stationed in garrisons along the rivers. During the fourth century, forts were established on the east bank of the Rhine in an effort to add another measure of security to the frontier in the face of the threat of incursions to the Roman settlements on the west bank. Among these were new bases at Mainz-Kastel, across the river from Mainz, and Köln-Deutz, across from Cologne. Fleets of warships played important roles during this period. They patrolled the river, providing an immediate physical defense against any invaders who might try to attack in boats crossing the Rhine. The Rhine at Mainz is considerably wider than the Danube at Regensburg. At its narrowest, the Rhine is about 450 yards wide today; it was likely wider in Roman times, before banks were built to control flooding during times of high water. The fleets were also responsible for supplying the troops stationed on both banks. And of course the ships ferried the soldiers back and forth across the Rhine as needed and transported them to points up or down the river where they were required.

Material remains of the fleet based at Mainz were discovered in the early 1980s when digging began for the construction of an annex to the Mainz Hilton. Between November 1981 and February 1982, archaeologists uncovered the remains of five Roman warships twenty-five feet below the modern ground surface. Associated objects indicate that the ships date to the fourth century. Their sinking has been linked by some investigators to invasions by groups from across the Rhine at the beginning of the fifth century (406–407). Three ships were too fragmentary to determine their original size. Of the two that were better preserved in the mud at the bottom of what apparently had been a harbor at the edge of the river, the larger was seventy-one feet long and nine feet wide. It accommodated thirty-two rowers and had a sail.

Archaeologists have identified some traces of what they interpret as destruction events during the fourth and early fifth centuries at Mainz, but the evidence is ambiguous; most importantly, it shows regular rebuilding. Hence it is not clear that the archaeology shows substantial destruction through invasion. Much of the evidence may simply reflect regular processes of urban renewal and rebuilding. During the fifth century, the Roman military presence gradually lessened all along the Rhine frontier, at Mainz and elsewhere. But for much of the city itself, the evidence shows that Roman buildings and the Roman urban layout continued to play vital roles in the city's life.

Significant commercial activity developed along the shore of the Rhine, accompanied by new construction associated with settlement activity and shops of industrial and commercial workers. Materials recovered on the site show important trade links with other regions during the seventh and eighth centuries. These links include substantial interactions with the growing industrial and commercial centers of the lower Rhine region, including the great trade port at Dorestad near the mouth of the Rhine, and with other expanding towns farther afield on the coasts of the English Channel, the North Sea, and the Baltic Sea (chapters 7 and 10).

COLOGNE

Like Regensburg and Mainz, Cologne was established as a military base and grew over time into a major civilian settlement, becoming the political capital of the two Roman provinces of Germany—Germania superior and Germania

Figure 5.6. Roman tower at Cologne, Germany. It is part of the wall, almost two miles long, that surrounded the city. Note the elaborate patterning in the bricks and stone.

inferior. As at Regensburg, much of the Roman city is still visible aboveground, including extensive sections of the perimeter wall. The Praetorium, the monumental stone building that served as the administrative center for the two provinces, is well preserved and displayed for visitors about two floors below the modern city hall.

At Cologne, as at Regensburg and Mainz, the archaeological evidence shows continuity from the Roman city to the medieval and modern cities. Early Christian church buildings were present as early as the fourth century, and Cologne soon became an important early center of the new religion (chapter 11). Habitation remains in the city and the cemeteries outside the city walls attest to the continuity of occupation at Cologne following the disintegration of the Roman army in the fifth century. A 470-yard-long stone bridge with oak pilings at its base was built across the Rhine, probably in the fourth century. Dendrochronological (tree ring) dating shows that some of the oak trees used in the foundations of the pillars were felled in the year A.D. 336, but it is not clear whether those trees were part of the original construction or of repairs made to an existing bridge. The bridge remained in use into the tenth century, when, according to one text, Archbishop Bruno of Cologne (953–965) ordered it dismantled.

The area of the city closest to the Rhine River, where the focus of the Roman urban center had been situated, remained the site of active manufacturing and commercial activity throughout the early Middle Ages without a break. During this period a cathedral and a royal palace were also situated here. As at other major Roman urban centers in Europe, as archaeological investigations are carried out beneath the modern city, more and more evidence attests to the continuity of occupation and substantial social and commercial activity from the Roman period into the medieval, instead of the break that had been supposed by earlier investigators who based their thinking on the scanty surviving written sources.

CONTINUITY AND CHANGE

As these examples indicate, major urban centers of the Roman Empire in Europe persisted as important central places throughout the times of reduction in Roman military presence. Building programs in Roman-style architecture ceased to be maintained, of course, but in many respects the basic character of urban life did not change. Patterns similar to those at the cities discussed above can be identified all over Roman Europe—for example, at Metz, Paris, Strasbourg, and Tours, in France; at Basel and Geneva, in Switzerland; at Konstanz, Passau, and Trier, in Germany; at Vienna, in Austria; at Ghent, in Belgium; and at London (chapter 6), Winchester, and York, in England. And these are only where good archaeological data now exist to demonstrate the continuity. This is not to say that no places of Roman importance declined in activity. There was a great deal of variation. But a general decline in cities and towns in the fourth and fifth centuries did not occur. In many prominent cases, urban life continued as vibrantly as before, but with a different character.

The centers that formed during the sixth, seventh, and eighth centuries—some of them in lands once ruled by Rome, some north and east of them—grew and thrived because there were always demands for goods that people could not produce for themselves. Some of these goods were fine craft products—such as ornate jewelry, decorated vessels, and special weapons—that could be made only by specialized crafts workers who were supported by people who produced food, clothing, and other necessities. But a great many of the goods that wealthy and powerful individuals demanded were luxury products that could be obtained only through long-distance trade. These included fine glassware, large amber ornaments, gold, and special crafts products that were made only in specialized regional workshops. More than any other single factor, the desire for, and the ability to pay for, such luxury goods on the part of wealthy individuals drove the development of urban centers. Some were on the sites of former Roman cities; others were within once-Roman territories but in new places (such as at Dinas Powys, in Wales; Tintagel, in Cornwall; Quentovic, in northern France; Maastricht, in the Netherlands; and Namur, in Belgium). A third group included new centers that developed far beyond the lands once controlled by Rome; they form the subject of chapter 7.

THE IDEA OF DECLINE AND THE BROADER PERSPECTIVE

This chapter has focused on what happened in the early medieval period at Rome itself and at three major Roman cities on the European frontier of the Empire. All show continuity of occupation into the fifth and sixth centuries, and indeed throughout the Middle Ages and into modern times. There is no evidence for contraction of the places or for population decline, even though the traditions of Roman architecture and road-building, and maintenance of aqueducts and sewers, effectively ceased with the end of official Roman administration in the fourth and fifth centuries. But in all cases, the archaeological evidence shows not only continuity of populations but use of Roman buildings and street arrangements long after the fifth and sixth centuries.

To speak of decline in these cities is to view the situation exclusively through the eyes of someone who believes unquestioningly that Roman traditions were superior to other—in this case local—cultural traditions. If we focus instead on the question of how people who lived in and around the cities adapted to the changing conditions in the world in which they lived and how they shaped those changes, we can appreciate the practices and indeed the achievements of the people who lived at the time.

Among the best-studied Roman and early medieval cities in the world is London, where the evidence for the growth of a new economic, political, and religious center in the Dark Ages is particularly informative.

6

Roman Londinium to Saxon Lundenwic: Continuity and Change (A.D. 43–800)

❖

ROMAN LONDON?

LONDON IS ONE OF THE MOST THOROUGHLY INVESTIGATED cities of the Roman Empire. That statement will come as a surprise to many people, whether they think of Londinium, the Roman period precursor to the modern city, as an outpost nine hundred miles northwest of the imperial capital, or whether they are unaware that London was ever part of the Empire. On hearing the name "London," the first images of most people who do not live in Britain are likely to be of Shakespeare and his theaters, the bobbies in their high hats, red double-decker buses, Carnaby Street and the "swinging" city of the 1960s, or a target of twenty-first-century terrorists. London was the largest and richest city of Roman Britain. Because of the extensive archaeological research that has been conducted on the Roman city of London, the existing city and its region provide an exceptionally good source of information for understanding what happened in the late Roman and early medieval periods.

If you spend a few days seeing the sights in London, chances are you will not encounter any ongoing archaeological excavations. When archaeologists investigate the rich layers of earth beneath the modern city, they must do so underneath mod-

Figure 6.1. Roman wall, London. This section was part of the easternmost portion of the city wall. It stands just north of the Tower of London, next to the Tower Hill underground (subway) station.

ern buildings or in the tight confines of building sites, which are ordinarily shut off from public access by fences. Except in the British Museum and especially in the Museum of London, where large quantities of archaeological finds are displayed along with reconstructions and maps, you are not likely to see anything of Roman date. But if you make an effort and know where to look, you will find remains of Roman period walls

Figure 6.2. Corner of Roman fort, London. This view on Noble Street shows part of the foundation of the fort in the northwestern corner of the Roman city. In the background are some of the later buildings that now cover this section of Londinium.

amidst the urban sprawl of modern London. Just north of the Tower of London, next to the Tower tube station, is a large section of the Roman city wall. On Noble Street, just south of the Museum of London, if you look down from sidewalk level you can see part of the fort that guarded the city wall at its northwestern corner, along with the foundation of one of the bastions. Recent excavations at the Guildhall in the center of the city revealed the Roman amphitheater, the remains of which are now open to visitors beneath the plaza in front of the Guildhall. The outline of the amphitheater is conveniently marked by colored stone on the plaza itself, so you can get a good impression of its size and position in relation to the layout of the modern city.

When you visit St. Paul's Cathedral, the Tower of London, the Old Bailey Law Courts, and the Guildhall, you are walking above Roman remains. If you should have business at the Bank of England or at Lloyd's, you will also be just above the foundations of the Roman city. The reason you do not see the Roman structures is that they are beneath layers of construction and habitation debris that has built up over the past two thousand years. In some places, the Roman remains lie as much as twenty feet beneath the current ground surface.

The shape of the Roman city still determines much of the fundamental structure of the modern British capital, particularly that part of London known today as "the City," where the financial (the Bank of England and the Stock Exchange) and religious (St. Paul's Cathedral) centers are still situated. If you glance at a modern map, you will see that major streets of the modern city trace most of the route of the Roman city walls. Just north of the Tower is Minories, then Camomile, Wormwood, and the major thoroughfare named, appropriately, London Wall. Where the Fleet River used to form the western

Figure 6.3. Outline of part of the Roman amphitheater, Guildhall, London. The shape of the amphitheater has been marked out in dark stone on the open space in front of the Guildhall. The stone foundations of the amphitheater lie two stories directly below.

Figure 6.4. View up Farringdon Street, London, looking north toward the bridge carrying Holborn Viaduct over the valley of the Fleet River. The river, which formed the western boundary of the Roman city, now flows underneath the street, and the valley is still very apparent in the topography of modern London. When the land was cleared to erect the modern buildings on the left side of Farringdon Street just north of the bridge, an important Roman cemetery was found at this location, which is just beyond the boundary of the city of Londinium.

boundary of the Roman city, Farringdon Street now runs over the stream, which is hidden from view below. Even today on Farringdon Street, you can get a good impression of the original topography of the area because the street is in a gully with steep sides to the east (the western edge of the Roman city) and to the west (where a Roman cemetery was situated beyond the city walls). The locations of the five principal gates in the Roman wall are still major parts of the urban road network—

from west to east, Ludgate, Newgate, Aldersgate, Bishopsgate, and Aldgate.

To get a firsthand feel for the size of the Roman city, I recently walked across its greatest width from west to east. It took twenty-five minutes at a brisk pace. That time included a few pauses for traffic lights, but surely in Roman London a pedestrian would have been slowed dodging horse-drawn carts and crowds of shoppers.

Of course, during the centuries after the Roman period, London expanded greatly beyond the bounds of the Roman walls, toward the west in the fifth through eighth centuries and in all directions in later medieval and modern times.

WHY HERE?

The place where the Roman army established London, and where the city stands today, was not a major center of economic or political activity before the arrival of the conquering Roman armies in A.D. 43. There was no lack of small-scale settlement and farming in the region from the Stone Age on, but the big centers of population and power at the time of the Roman invasion lay elsewhere. The late Iron Age centers included Colchester, to the northeast; St. Albans, to the northwest; Bagendon, to the west; and Silchester, to the southwest. But the natural geography of the site that was to become London offered important advantages.

Shortly after Roman armies under the emperor Claudius invaded Britain in A.D. 43, Roman authorities established a military and civil base where London now stands. The site was chosen for three reasons of geography of movement, involving the river, the sea, and land routes.

At London, the river Thames is, and was, deep enough to

accommodate seagoing ships. The site is situated about thirty miles from the North Sea, and at London the Thames is tidal. Ship captains could benefit by riding the tide. They could sail upsteam with the help of the rising tide, and could travel easily downstream and out into the North Sea on the falling tide. When the Roman authorities began to build their city here, the Thames was quite different from the modern river. It was some 330 yards wide (now 110 yards) at low tide, and sometimes more than 1,100 yards wide at high tide (at high tide today, the Thames is 250 yards wide at London Bridge). Because of the wider bed, the river was correspondingly shallower and slower flowing than it is now.

Such ready access to the sea meant easy communications with the rest of the Roman Empire—with Gaul, just across the English Channel, and more distant places such as Rome and North Africa via the North Atlantic, the Strait of Gibraltar, and the Mediterranean.

London is at the farthest point downstream on the Thames where the river could be bridged easily with the technology available to the Roman engineers. Its location was already on routes of communication in the pre-Roman period; so in bridging the river, the Roman founders were able to exploit and expand an existing road network.

The original Roman military and civil settlement was on a gravel terrace covered with a layer of clay on the north bank of the Thames. The terrace, as high as fifty feet above the surface of the Thames, provided security against flooding. Through the middle of this terrace, the Walbrook flowed southward in a shallow gully; to the west, the terrace was bounded by the larger Fleet River. The mouths of these two streams offered convenient harbors for small boats. The south bank of the Thames was low, marshy land that was not developed until later.

Figure 6.5. Reconstruction view of Roman London, showing the city as it probably looked during the early second century. At the upper left is the Fleet River (now covered by Farringdon Street), which formed the western boundary of the city. In the center background is the fort, with its square enclosing wall and long barracks. The amphitheater is just in front of the fort. In the middle of the densest part of the city are the forum and the

basilica, then the largest structure north of the Alps. The Walbrook can be seen flowing through the middle of the city, its confluence into the Thames about halfway between the western edge of the built-up area and the bridge. The bridge allowed the expansion of the Roman city onto the south bank of the Thames, which was a low-lying and marshy area.

THRIVING LONDINIUM (A.D. 90–350)

The Roman settlement at London is believed to have been started by the army, shortly after the Roman invasion of Britain in A.D. 43, to establish a base at an important crossing point on the Thames. Sometime during the second half of the first century, the first bridge was constructed. In the first two decades, the population is thought to have been between 5,000 and 10,000. By the end of the first century, the population of the Roman settlement was between 20,000 and 30,000, made up of soldiers, crafts workers, merchants, administrators, and others. The majority were indigenous Britons or their descendants, though the thriving town attracted immigrants from abroad, and of course army commanders and the most important administrators were sent by Rome. Already in the latter part of the first century, Roman administrators decided to make Londinium the principal city of Britain and began a program of large-scale public architecture. Paved streets were laid out, up to thirty feet wide in some places; a forum and basilica were built; and an amphitheater, baths, and temples were constructed of cut stone, a medium that Iron Age builders in the region had not used. In the northwestern corner of the walled enclosure, a fort was built that housed the soldiers who guarded the city.

The late first and second centuries were the time of peak prosperity for Roman London. Between A.D. 90 and 200, Londinium must have been an exciting and flourishing place. Wharves constructed along the north bank of the Thames provided berth for ships arriving from all parts of the Empire, bearing a wide range of foodstuffs, luxury utensils, ornaments, and raw materials. Archaeological finds attest to the importation of great quantities of wine, in ceramic amphoras and wooden barrels, from Italy, Spain, and the Rhineland of Germany. Other amphoras carried olive oil, important for cooking and lighting, and the fish sauce known as *garum,* of which Romans were fond (probably something like Worcestershire sauce today). Olives, dates, figs, pomegranates, almonds, and pine nuts have also been identified. A variety of herbs and spices were imported. Livestock, fish, and grains were brought from different sources into the port to feed the urban population.

Among manufactured goods, fine pottery was imported in great quantities from Gaul, the Rhineland, and elsewhere, including the fine, hard-fired red tableware known as terra sigillata, frequently decorated with scenes in relief. Bronze vessels and ceramic lamps came from Italy, and fine glass vessels from the Rhineland, Italy, and lands of the eastern Mediterranean. Bronze ornaments and ceramic figurines were brought from the continent, and prized substances that were imported include amber from the southern shores of the Baltic Sea and emeralds from Egypt. Fine marble for carving tombstones, furniture, and ornaments came from quarries in Mediterranean lands, and massive grindstones made of basalt were brought from the Mayen region, on the west bank of the middle Rhine. Goods were unloaded from the ships and stored in warehouses that lined the waterfront on both sides of the Thames, and other goods from the warehouses were loaded onto the ships.

Britain's exports, many of which were transported through the bustling port of Londinium, included metals, special stone, and slaves. Lead was mined in Derbyshire and the Mendip Hills in Somerset. Tin was extracted from mines in Cornwall. Dorset marble was quarried to make fine grinding implements, such as mortars and pestles and palettes for preparing cosmetics. Shale from Dorset was made into household items and jewelry. Jet from Yorkshire served as raw material for ornaments such as beads and bracelets. The trade in slaves was always important in the Roman world, though it is usually difficult to discern in the archaeological evidence. It is likely that slaves captured in wars on the northern frontier beyond Hadrian's Wall were traded through the port of London to other parts of the Empire.

Londinium's streets were bustling with carts carrying grain, produce, and meat from the farms beyond the city walls to the central marketplace at the forum. Storefront shops lined many of the streets, and potential customers haggled with shopkeepers over the price of goods.

Archaeological investigations have revealed houses of several different kinds. At one extreme were simple huts built of posts sunk into the ground forming the corners, with wattle-and-daub walls and dirt floors. Wattle-and-daub architecture consists of thin branches (the wattle), half an inch to an inch in diameter, bent to fit around the vertical posts, with clay plaster (the daub) packed between and over the branches on both sides to keep out wind and moisture. This technique of house building was widespread from Neolithic times in many parts of the world, and it remains in use in some places today. This was the type of house in which the majority of the population of Roman Britain lived.

At the other extreme were the homes of wealthy merchants and administrators appointed by Rome. Their houses were built of stone and had roofs made of fired ceramic tiles. The walls were plastered and whitewashed, and inside often painted with landscape scenes and other decorations. Some of the rooms had colorful mosaic floors. These houses were centrally heated, with open spaces under the floors warmed by air heated by fires in the basement. The hot air circulated under the tile floors and was forced up through channels in the walls to provide respite from the damp cold of the British winter.

The contrast between the small wattle-and-daub huts in which most people lived and the great stone, plaster, and tile houses of the wealthy, with their painted walls and decorative mosaics, indicates the differences between groups within early European societies. By the Neolithic period (from about 4000 B.C. in Britain), differences in status and wealth were well established. These show up most clearly in burials, where a few individuals were buried with lavish grave goods consisting of ornate pottery and gold ornaments, whereas the majority of people had only the most rudimentary burial items or none at all. In the late Iron Age (from 100 B.C. to the Roman conquest in A.D. 43), special status was displayed through richly outfitted graves that included many ceramic vessels of fine ware, some imported from Roman Italy and Gaul; bronze and silver vessels; and quantities of bronze and gold jewelry. The differences in status and wealth expressed in burial goods carry into the Roman period, when much greater quantities of material luxuries became available. We can understand the disparities in wealth as proxies for differences in power, influence, and opportunity, just as we see in later times. Although the archaeological evidence does not reveal the nuances of the privileges and authority represented by the great wealth associated with some individuals, it is clear that the elites lived different lives from those of the majority of the people.

Like the political and commercial elites in all major Roman cities, the elites of Londinium expressed their power and status through public monumental architecture. The huge stone wall that surrounded the city, enclosing 330 acres of land, was different from anything that the native Britons had ever seen, and it made a strong impression on them. The baths, amphitheater, and temples were grandiose buildings constructed of carved imported stone and on a scale much larger than their functions required. More than five hundred feet long and probably some eighty-five feet high, the basilica was the largest building north of the Alps during the second and third centuries and a monumental symbol of the political and economic might of this Roman provincial capital. It was constructed of gray stone and red brick, and its roof was red tile. The basilica housed what we would call the city hall, government administrative offices, and courts. Next to this massive building on its south side was the forum, a large open area surrounded by long narrow structures that probably housed shops. The forum served as the principal market of the city and as a general public meeting place.

CEMETERIES

We learn a great deal about the people who lived in Roman London from their graves. In addition to the physical remains of the people, items placed in the graves with the deceased provide important evidence about the objects available to Londoners and about burial practices among this urban population. Visiting London today, it is difficult to imagine that any cemeteries from the Roman city survive. But in the course of modern construction, graves are regularly uncovered and carefully excavated and analyzed.

In the Roman world, it was common practice to place cemeteries outside city walls. At many Roman urban centers, cemeteries line the roads just outside the city gates. In the early years of Roman London, cremation was the practice favored throughout much of the Empire. Typical in first-century

London was placement of the ashes and burned bone fragments in a ceramic, glass, or metal urn, sometimes with a small ceramic vessel or an item or two of jewelry, and burial of the urn in a hole in the ground. During the second century A.D., inhumation gained in favor. Usually the deceased was laid out in an extended position, often with a few objects added before the grave was filled in. By the end of the third century, inhumation was the dominant rite. In contrast to the situation in many parts of pre-Roman Europe, in Roman contexts the practice was to place very few objects in graves with the dead. Gravestones with inscriptions about the deceased individual marked some graves, but only those of elites.

By the sixteenth century, discovery of Roman graves in and around London was being noted in historical records, and from then to the present, cemeteries have been uncovered all around the Roman walls, even on the south bank of the Thames. Among the larger cemeteries investigated in recent times is one situated east of Aldgate on the east side of the walls. More than 800 burials could be identified in this cemetery, 550 of them containing inhumations, 136 cremations, and others disturbed by subsequent digging in the area.

A particularly interesting grave was discovered during construction work on March 15, 1999, in the area of London known as Spitalfields, just northeast of the Roman city. When discovered by archaeologists working in advance of construction crews, the grave was undisturbed. Inside a stone sarcophagus was a coffin made of lead and decorated with a pattern of scallop shells. The coffin contained the skeleton of a woman in her early twenties; she was five feet four inches tall. She had been wrapped in a textile, and under her head was a pillow containing bay leaves. Textile fragments recovered indicate the presence of silk from China, wool, and gold thread. Placed between the coffin and the wall of the sarcophagus was a glass vessel, and another was in the grave pit but outside the sarcophagus. Other grave goods included a rod made of jet, a cylindrical box, a flat ring of jet, and a jet pin. The style of the objects allows archaeologists to date this grave to around A.D. 350. The grave goods, the carved limestone sarcophagus, and the ornate lead coffin indicate that this young woman was a person of considerable status and wealth, and the grave provides a good demonstration that high-status persons with access to lavish luxury goods were still active at London as late as the middle of the fourth century.

THE LIVES OF THE PEOPLE

Analysis of the skeletons in London's cemeteries enables physical anthropologists to learn much about health, nutrition, and stature of Roman period Londoners. The bones indicate that overall nutrition was good. Remains of foods recovered through archaeological excavation indicate the extraordinary variety of foods available—a much greater variety than had been available to pre-Roman populations of Britain. Besides the Iron Age staples of cattle and cereal grains, pork and chicken played greater roles in the diet during the Roman period. Fish of various kinds, both marine and riverine, and oysters were consumed in great quantities. Among legumes, lentils and peas are well represented in archaeological finds. Grape and fig seeds have been recovered in many parts of the city, and other fruits present were apple, pear, plum, and cherry. Wild game and nuts were also consumed but in smaller quantities. We do not yet know enough about what proportion of Londoners had access to all or most of these foods to say whether or not imported items such as figs were restricted to wealthy individuals, but it is clear that the city as a whole had a tremendous diversity of foods available.

Relatively few severe injuries show up on the bones of those buried in the London cemeteries, suggesting that violence in the city was not a serious problem. Dental health was generally good, corresponding with the good diet and some degree of dental hygiene. A small number of skeletons show traces of tuberculosis, a disease that sometimes spreads in environments where diet is not as good and people live in overcrowded situations. Apparently for some Londoners, life was not as healthy as it was for others.

The worst off of London's residents were the slaves. An integral part of the Roman economy, as they had been in Greece, slaves did much of the menial work with minimal compensation. Slaves were ordinarily individuals who were captured in war, or descendents of prisoners of war. Slavery in the Roman world was complex. Slaves could acquire wealth of their own, purchase slaves for themselves, and, with luck and hard work, buy their freedom.

A particularly interesting, though disturbing, written document attesting to the sale of a young slave in London was unearthed in 1994 in the course of major excavations at 1 Poultry, opposite the Bank of England and the Stock Exchange. A thin tablet of silver fir, $5\frac{1}{2}$ inches by $4\frac{1}{2}$ inches in size, originally covered on one surface with wax, had legible traces of writing done with a sharp stylus incised into the wood. Only through unusual circumstances of moisture and acidity did this delicate wooden object survive. The Latin text records the sale of a girl named Fortunata who came from Gaul, across the English Channel. The sale took place around A.D. 100, at the peak of Londinium's prosperity. The buyer was a man named Vegetus,

Figure 6.6. View looking west from the intersection at the heart of the financial center of London, where the Bank of England and the Stock Exchange are located. This was also a center of economic activity in the Roman city. Abundant archaeological remains were found at the site of the new building in the center background, at 1 Poultry.

who was a government official and a slave himself. The slave girl cost six hundred denari. (The annual salary of a legionary soldier in the Roman army was about half this amount.)

Measurements taken on skeletons from the cemeteries around London show that Londoners of the Roman period were only slightly shorter than modern inhabitants of the United Kingdom. Average heights for men were about five feet six inches and for women about five feet two inches. A man buried in a grave found near modern Giltspur Street stood six feet two inches tall.

RELIGION AND RITUAL

Roman cities typically had numerous temples dedicated to the worship of the principal gods and goddesses of the Roman pantheon. In the modern city, it is of course difficult to get a full overview of the locations of the different ritual precincts of the Roman metropolis. In excavations conducted in 1975 along the riverside wall of the Roman city, several significant sculpted stones related to religious themes were recovered. They included an altar used for the worship of Jupiter, the chief among the gods of Rome. Also found was a carved stone showing four mother goddesses, deities connected to pre-Roman (Celtic) beliefs and practices rather than to Roman ones. All are shown robed in body-length textiles and holding fruits and bread, symbols of fertility and nurturing. Much other evidence for religion and ritual in Roman period London attests to the wide diversity of belief and practice among the people of this cosmopolitan center.

Like the Fleet River, the Walbrook—which once played an important role in the city—is now covered by a modern street. Excavations conducted since the 1870s have recovered a wide array of objects that Roman period Londoners deposited into this stream. Quantities of human skulls were found—more than a hundred of them at one location near modern Blomfield Street, just north of the Roman city wall; most dated to the first two centuries A.D. Also recovered were large numbers of iron and bronze objects—knives and other implements, jewelry, spoons, coins, and styli (pointed objects used for writing on wooden tablets coated with wax). The Walbrook finds belong to a large group of water deposits from prehistoric and Roman period northern Europe, where objects were offered to gods as votive gifts. This practice survives today in the tradition of tossing coins into wells or fountains. At Bath, in the southwest of England, and at the military fort at Vindolanda on Hadrian's Wall, in the north, metal tablets have been found that bear inscriptions attesting to this purpose for depositing valuable objects in water.

On the east bank of the Walbrook was found one of the most interesting structures in all of Roman London. In clearing debris in 1954 left from World War II bomb damage, construction workers came upon the structural remains of what turned out to be a well-preserved Mithraeum—a semi-subterranean temple used for the worship of the god Mithras. Mithras is believed to have originally been a god of ancient Persia (now Iran), but his worship was taken up by many groups throughout the Roman Empire. Mithras was a sun god and had special connections to cattle and snakes. Remains of the cult of Mithras are especially abundant along the frontiers of the Roman Empire, in northern Britain along Hadrian's Wall, and along the Rhine and the Danube frontiers. The cult of Mithras was especially popular during the second and third centuries. Several hundred temples to Mithras are known from the Roman world, and many more inscriptions associated with his cult have been identified.

The Mithraeum on the Walbrook in London was constructed around the middle of the third century. It consisted of a long hall with columns on either side and with the cult image of Mithras slaying a bull, in a scene that included the familiar signs of the zodiac, at the far end. Archaeological investigation of the temple revealed several phases of rebuilding. The temple went out of use sometime in the fourth century. Interestingly, the sculptures that were part of the ritual celebrations in the temple were carefully buried in pits on the site. These included marble heads of Mithras himself and the associated god Serapis, both preserved intact because they were safely buried out of harm's way. This means of "disposing" of religious sculptures surely does not reflect destruction by rival successors, which probably would have involved smashing or at least defacing the sculptures. The fate of the London Mithraeum in the fourth century corresponds to what was going on in much of the city at that time.

DECLINE OF ROMAN LONDON?

After the glory days of Roman Londinium in the first and second centuries, the character of the city changed. Textual sources indicate that in A.D. 410, the Roman central administration told the officials in Britain that they had to manage their own defenses against the forces trying to destroy them; the government in Rome could send no more troops. To understand what happened between the thriving second-century metropolis and the relinquishing of Roman control in A.D. 410, and further changes in the cultural landscape during the fifth and sixth centuries, we are dependent upon the material evidence of archaeology.

Beginning in the third century and continuing into the fourth, there is clear evidence for major changes in what people were doing in the city. Two changes are particularly evident, one involving the reuse of stone architectural elements, the other the deposition of soil over much of the formerly built-up urban area.

DISMANTLING MONUMENTS

During the third and fourth centuries, some large public structures built of stone were allowed to fall into disrepair, whereas others were carefully taken down, apparently for reuse of the stone elsewhere. Some of the stone was employed for building a new wall along the north bank of the Thames. Excavations in the 1970s in Upper Thames Street, along the course of the Roman river wall and the bank of the Thames at that time (the edge of the river is now about one hundred yards south of this), recovered sculpted stones and fifty-two blocks of cut stone that had been parts of standing structures. Some of the sculpted stones, carved with floral ornament and images of deities, had formed parts of a monumental arch. Others, also with images of deities carved in relief, were parts of a tableau, or screen, twenty feet in length. Separate blocks of stone included the sculpture of four mother goddesses, mentioned above, and two altars. Dating of the river wall of which these stones formed parts, with both dendrochronology and radiocarbon, indicates that it was built sometime during the second half of the fourth century.

Some stones removed from large public structures were used for building houses for wealthy individuals during the third and fourth centuries. Blocks of cut stone that had been part of the great monuments such as the basilica, the temples, and the amphitheater were removed from those structures and reused for other building projects. Even sculptures such as statues and tombstones were recycled as building stone. In the display of Roman materials in the Museum of London, much of the sculpture in the galleries had been reused as building stone. This practice of dismantling buildings to procure the stone blocks, and removing statues and gravestones to use the material for construction, seems strange to us, but it was common practice in the late Roman period and is well documented at many cities during the fourth century.

The question that we need to ask is, what had happened?

What were these people thinking and intending as they dismantled elaborately constructed, ornate buildings and sculptures that included religious representations? What is the meaning of this change—from valuing the monumental stone buildings and the representational sculpture to exploiting these essential features of Roman culture merely for their raw material? We need to understand these actions in terms of new kinds of uses of the urban space that had been the thriving city of Londinium.

DARK EARTH

The third and fourth centuries at London are characterized by the widespread presence of dark humic soil, sometimes more than a yard thick and with cultural debris (pottery, bones of butchered animals, glass fragments) mixed into it, covering occupational remains of the earlier centuries. This material, known as dark earth, is not unique to London but has been identified at many urban sites all over northern Europe during late Roman times. There has been a great deal of discussion and debate about this dark earth—what it represents and how it originated. It was once widely regarded as evidence of decline and abandonment of Roman urban centers. It was considered a natural soil that developed on top of areas that had once been active parts of the urban center, such as we might observe forming in a vacant lot in a city today.

For a variety of reasons, this interpretation has changed. The dark earth is now thought to represent not abandonment but rather thriving activity—but activity of a very different character from that of the Roman urban centers. The dark earth has been found to contain remains of timber-framed, wattle-and-daub huts, along with sherds of pottery and metal ornaments datable to the late Roman period. These observations demonstrate that people who were living on the site were building their houses in the traditional British style rather than in the stone and cement fashion of elite and public Roman architecture. Such structures are much more difficult to identify in the archaeological material than Roman stone buildings, because all that is typically left of them are postholes in the ground and crumbly fragments of the daub that had been packed around the branchwork of the walls.

What are we to make of these two major changes reflected in the archaeology? After rapid growth in the latter part of the first century, London emerged as a stunning center of the Roman Empire on its northern edge, with the monumental architecture, a thriving commercial center, and a military base characteristic of the greatest of Roman cities. The third and fourth centuries at London are marked by a stoppage in major public architecture and a reverse of that process, the dismantling of major stone monuments, at the same time that much of the formerly urban area seems to have reverted to a non-urban character.

To call these changes "decline," "collapse," or "abandonment"—as has been done in the past—is to adopt a conservative Roman attitude toward change. Because we live in societies that use monumental stone architecture in ways similar to how Rome used it, we tend to think of dismantling such structures—our monuments to military and civic glory—as distasteful. But the question we need to ask is, how can we understand these changes in terms of the lives and actions of the inhabitants of this specific place?

All of these changes—the dismantling of stone buildings, the reuse of the stone, and the buildup of the dark earth—

can be understood in terms of new uses of the formerly urban landscape for different purposes. As evidence accumulates in London, it is becoming clear that the site was not abandoned, as earlier researchers had thought. Life went on in place throughout the third, fourth, and fifth centuries; it was just different. For reasons that are explored below, the inhabitants of London after the glory years of the second century did not have uses for the monumental stone structures that played such important roles between A.D. 70 and 200. Their needs were different, and they behaved in ways dictated by their traditions and their uses of the resources available to them.

CONTINUITY INTO THE MIDDLE AGES—SAXON LUNDENWIC

In the traditional framework, a distinction is made between Roman London and Saxon London, with finer distinctions between Early and Late Roman and Early, Middle, and Late Saxon. In earlier traditions of research, these categories had some value as means for organizing accumulating information, but the use of such categories also hinders thinking about broad patterns of continuity. In fact, until the mid-1980s, when archaeological excavation began on the site of the Royal Opera House at Covent Garden, there was little evidence for Early Saxon activity in London at all.

The beginning of the Saxon period in London is traditionally defined as the time when material culture designated as Germanic became abundant, during the fifth and sixth centuries. Until a couple of decades ago, it was believed that a clear topographical separation existed between the Roman city in what is now the City of London on the north bank of the Thames, between the Fleet River and the Tower of London, and the post-Roman Saxon settlement to the west, where the Thames bends from flowing northward to flowing eastward, just downstream from Westminster. Recent discoveries have greatly complicated this picture.

Objects classified as Germanic have been recovered within the Roman city. Examples include a chip-carved bronze belt buckle made around A.D. 400 found at Smithfield, and several sixth-century bronze brooches recovered from Lower Thames Street and at Tower Hill. Conversely, Roman objects have been found in the early medieval settlement area around Covent Garden. These include fourth-century Roman coins, a brooch in the shape of a dolphin, other ornaments, and numerous tiles reused as pavings in various contexts. The significance of these finds is that we can no longer be content with the neatly delineated Roman city to the east and the Saxon settlement to the west. It is now apparent that since the time when the first Roman settlement was established in the area in the mid-first-century A.D., there has been considerable habitation, manufacturing, industrial, and construction activity on the north bank of the Thames, and it did not let up from early Roman times to the present day.

When dealing with a large modern urban center, it is always important to remember that the only archaeological evidence that we can collect is what happens to have been preserved and happens to be situated in places where modern construction activity exposes layers belowground. When a new subway line is put in or a new office tower is constructed, archaeologists have an opportunity to investigate archaeological layers preserved beneath the modern city. It is a very different situation from exploring an ancient settlement that is no longer the site of a great urban complex. At abandoned sites such as

Troy in Turkey, Teotihuacan in Mexico, and Cahokia in Illinois, archaeologists are able to explore parts of the site that they think might contain important remains. Based on the scattered and random (in the sense that the archaeologist cannot plan where to dig) distribution of archaeological materials from early London, the archaeologist attempts to reconstruct a picture of what the city was like two thousand years ago and how it changed.

Figure 6.7. Royal Opera House, Covent Garden (left), in a view looking northwest. During excavations in preparation for the expansion of this complex, archaeologists uncovered extensive remains of the Saxon settlement of London. A wide road was found, with alleys extending from it, as well as buildings of wattle-and-daub, and abundant remains of craft activity in metals, bone, and textiles.

The recent excavations at the site of the Royal Opera House (1989–1999), just northeast of Covent Garden Market, have revealed for the first time an extensive settlement area occupied during the sixth, seventh, and eighth centuries and continuing without interruption into modern times. This was the Saxon settlement known as Lundenwic. The community was actively involved in manufacturing and trade. Ironworking was practiced, as was the manufacture of jewelry of silver and gold. Wine bottles from abroad attest to the importation of wine. Workshops of butchers, hide tanners, and bone and horn carvers have been identified. The area of modern London around Covent Garden is now known to have been the site of a major settlement during this early medieval period. Excavations have revealed numerous house foundations, ditches, and storage pits and substantial evidence for manufacturing and commercial activity. Indications of industry include kilns for firing pottery, decorative pins of different kinds, combs made from antler, and loom weights attesting to weaving on the site. West of Covent Garden, where Trafalgar Square now is located, were farms that produced the foodstuffs for the crafts workers and merchants. Food remains in the Covent Garden settlement indicate that wheat, barley, and rye were particularly important in the diet of the people there, along with the meat from cattle, sheep, and pigs. Other foods included beans, hazelnuts, and berries and other fruits. Particularly well represented among trade goods are imported pottery from the continent and other parts of Britain, grindstones made of basalt from the middle Rhineland, and coins from many different places.

Many objects provide important indications that persons of high status and wealth were active in London during this period. An ornate silver sword hilt, partially gilded, found at Fetter Lane, was part of someone's highly prestigious weapon set during the latter part of the eighth century. A gold brooch

Figure 6.8. Trafalgar Square and St. Martin-in-the-Fields church (center). Remains of early Saxon farms have been found beneath Trafalgar Square. Excavations associated with recent renovations to the church of St. Martin-in-the-Fields have uncovered important burials of the late Roman period and of early Anglo-Saxon times.

with garnet inlay found at Floral Street was likely worn by a wealthy and influential woman. A seventh-century gold finger ring was found near Euston Square and another at Garrick Street; two gold earrings were found just northwest of the former center of Roman Londinium; and two glass cups were recovered at St. Martin-in-the-Fields, the church at the northeastern corner of Trafalgar Square.

The new finds show that, rather than thinking of the Roman settlement to the east in the City and the Saxon town in the West End of modern London, we need to think of the entire north bank of the river as the location of an extensive settlement whose inhabitants were engaged in a high level of economic activity across a broad riverside landscape.

Perhaps key to understanding what happened in London is the difference in architectural traditions between the grandiose, ostentatious stone buildings of imperial Rome and the traditional European wood-and-plaster architecture of the native peoples. All of the grand public architecture, and the first phase of the city walls, were constructed during a relatively brief period, between A.D. 70 and 200, when not just London but all of the Roman Empire in Europe flourished. The lack of such public architecture from the third century on, the dismantling of stone structures for the building of private residences and the river wall during the third and fourth centuries, and the proliferation of European-style timber-frame buildings that contributed to the formation of the dark earth do not reflect abandonment of the site or even decline in population and economic activity; rather these attest to changes in the character of settlement structures and functions. These physical changes are the material manifestations of transformation in the style of living of the residents of the place—from Roman architecture of stone and cement, with mosaics, wall paintings, and other accoutrements of the Mediterranean lifestyle, to buildings of native British character, similar to those of the pre-Roman Iron Age and the post-Roman Migration period.

To most residents of modern cities, this change from stone architecture of the early Roman period to wattle-and-daub of early medieval times might seem to be a shift to a more primitive way of life. But that reaction is based on our own familiarity with Roman-style (stone, concrete) architecture in our cities and on our bias that such architecture is more advanced than wood-and-plaster structures. If we think instead of the return—after the fourth century—to the traditional building techniques of native Britain as a matter of cultural choice rather than a result of impoverishment, we would be much closer to the mark. Many early medieval kings lived in palaces constructed using these architectural techniques, and some such buildings show evidence of considerable wealth during this period (the clearest example is the king's hall at Gudme in Denmark [chapter 7]). The rapidly accumulating signs of high status and great wealth from early medieval London, such as the gilded sword hilt and gold rings noted above (and these are only items that were lost and not found again for more than a thousand years!), attest to the fact that individuals of elite status resided there in the absence of Roman-style architecture.

It has been suggested that the apparent shift of the center of settlement activity from the old Roman city to the new location to the west was largely a result of practical considerations. The stone-and-cement foundations within the Roman city may have been impediments to the expansion of a settlement based on timber-frame architecture. The beaches along the north bank of the Thames just west of the Roman city would have offered more suitable landing places for pulling the flat-bottomed local trading boats up onto shore, unobstructed by the wooden structures that Roman engineers had erected along the waterfront of Londinium and that were now decaying.

Everything in London suggests continuity of occupation and economic activity along a broad swath of land north of the Thames throughout the first millennium. The center of gravity shifted over time, but there was no break in the lives of most Londoners. This picture that has emerged from the archaeological evidence over the past couple of decades is well supported by the existing textual records. From them we know that Pope Gregory made London a primatial see of England in 601, indicating that the place must have been important then. An Episcopal church was established in 604 at the site where St. Paul's Cathedral now stands. Written sources and the evidence of minted coins show that London was a thriving commercial center during the seventh, eighth, and ninth centuries. Texts refer to the existence of a king's hall at London in the final third of the seventh century. Other texts attest to major fires in the town in the years 764, 798, and 801, strongly suggesting a densely built-up urban area.

Once established as an urban and commercial center following the advance of the Roman legions into Britain in A.D. 43, London continued to flourish, even during times of major political and economic change, to the present day. Other centers in northern Europe were first established during the Dark Ages, and many of them continued to grow and thrive throughout the medieval period and into modern times.

7
New Centers in the North

❖

WHEN THE MISSIONARY ANSGAR ARRIVED AT BIRKA IN central Sweden,

> King Björn received them cordially . . . Many of the people were eager to hear [Ansgar's] message [about the new religion]. Numerous Christians lived there as slaves . . . Soon a chapel was built.
>
> At the trade port of Birka, there were many well-to-do merchants, an abundance of goods of all kinds, and much money and treasure.

These quotations give us important information about one of the new centers that grew rapidly in northern Europe and radically changed the political, cultural, and economic character of the continent. The quotes are from the biography of the mis-

Figure 7.1. Places mentioned in chapters 7 to 11.

sionary Ansgar, later Bishop of Hamburg, describing his visit to the northern trade port of Birka, on an island in Lake Mälaren in central Sweden. His visit was in the year 829, and the circumstances described are similar to those of the preceding century.

Three points in these quotations are especially significant. First, this growing trade center was ruled by a king, indicating that it was part of a large and complex political entity. Second, Christian slaves were part of the community, implying that traders in the north had captured persons farther south, perhaps in France, Germany, or Anglo-Saxon England, who were already Christian; or perhaps the traders obtained them from merchants based in those lands. Third, the words in the last sentence indicate that the commercial activity at this site must have been very active. This biography of Ansgar was written by his successor, Rimbert, who was also based at Hamburg. Hamburg was a substantial trading city by this time, and if Rimbert tells us that Birka had "many well-to-do merchants" and "an abundance of goods of all kinds," the commercial activity there must have been large-scale indeed.

This vivid description written by someone of the time gives us a feel for how the people of northern Europe regarded the growing centers in their midst. But for the earlier phases of development of Birka and most of the numerous other centers in northern Europe between 400 and 800, we have no written sources—only the material evidence of archaeology. In a sense, this lack of historical information and our need to rely on the archaeological data are key aspects of these new developments. The late Roman writers and most of their Dark Age successors knew nothing about these newly emerged centers (or if they did know, they chose not to mention them). But recent archaeological research tells us a detailed story about the dynamic development of new towns in northern Europe—towns that were to have an immense impact on subsequent European history.

GUDME

During the second century, around the time of peak prosperity for Roman cities and towns such as Regensburg, Mainz,

Cologne, and London, new centers of population and commerce were emerging in northern parts of the continent. These places were different in character from the Roman-style cities and towns of the provinces; they lacked the stone and cement or brick architecture of Mediterranean and provincial cityscapes. But in their regions, they came to play similar roles as political, economic, and ritual centers.

The best documented of these places is Gudme, in the southeastern part of the Danish island of Fyn, situated three miles inland from the coast. Indications that this place was becoming a central location of some importance appeared in the first and second centuries A.D., with unusually large numbers of imports from the Roman world in graves in the great cemetery of Møllegårdsmarken. In the third century, a major commercial and industrial site was established on the coast just east of Gudme, at Lundeborg; it served as the place of importation for a wide range of goods coming in from the outside world to the growing center at Gudme. Throughout the third and fourth centuries, quantities of goods from the Roman world arrived at Lundeborg, including especially fine pottery (terra sigillata) and glass in the form of vessels and beads, as well as Roman silver coins. We know about the importation of these objects at Lundeborg because of glass beads that were dropped and now found and because of the fragmentary remains of pottery and glass vessels that were discarded. No doubt quantities of other Roman goods, such as bronze vessels, also passed through the port, but because they did not break in transit, they did not leave direct evidence at this spot.

The Lundeborg port settlement, which extended about a thousand yards along the coast, was also a center of industrial activity. Extensive remains of ironworking are evident, as well as remains of the processing of bronze, silver, and gold. Amber, bone, and antler were carved in workshops on the site. Iron tools suggest that shipbuilding was carried out here. From the third to the end of the seventh century, Lundeborg was the site of intensive manufacturing activity and long-distance commerce.

During this same period, Gudme, three miles to the west, thrived as a center of commercial, political, and religious activity. An enormous hall—the largest structure in northern Europe during this period—stood near the center of the Gudme settlement complex. This extraordinary building was 154 feet long and 33 feet wide. Unusual quantities of gold ornaments and coins found in and around it indicate its special importance in the political and economic life of this place. The great diversity of imported objects also attests to the political and economic significance of this northern center. These objects include bronze vessels, statuary, and personal ornaments as well as fine pottery from the Roman world through the fourth century, gold and other precious ornaments from southeastern Europe during the fourth and fifth centuries, and personal ornaments from central and western Europe during the fifth and sixth centuries.

The large quantities of gold and of Roman objects that were deposited in graves, in hoards, and in houses at Gudme suggest that this center was different in its fundamental character from Roman towns in the provinces. Taking Gudme—and the contemporary center at Uppåkra, in southern Sweden—into consideration, it is clear that we need to thoroughly rethink our notions of what constituted a town or city in the first millennium in northern Europe. What combination of demographic, political, ritual, and economic factors made an urban center? The only way for us to understand the early medieval centers of temperate Europe is to develop a conception that includes the earlier Roman urban character, the new features that slowly emerged as the "Romanness" waned, and the new towns in the north that were established well beyond the former Roman territories. In the tightly interconnected commercial centers of the Middle Ages, all of these components need to be given their due weight, and the interactions between them closely examined for what they can tell us about changes that were taking place all over the continent.

A whole series of other trade towns in northern Europe of the period of Gudme and Lundeborg have been identified, but so far only limited excavation work has taken place at them. They include Dankirke, on the west coast of Jutland; Sorte Muld, on the Danish island of Bornholm; and Stentinget, in northern Jutland. By the late seventh century, a major trade center was developing at Ribe, on the west coast of Jutland just north of Dankirke.

HELGÖ

Situated on an island in Lake Mälaren, in central Sweden, just west of the modern city of Stockholm, Helgö was established as a major center of manufacturing and trade around A.D. 400. The industrial evidence recovered at the site shows that intensive metalworking and other crafts were carried out here. The extent of the trade networks of which the community at Helgö was a part is evident in the recovery there of a bronze figure of Buddha from northern India and an ornate bishop's crozier from Ireland. Chapter 9 deals with Helgö's manufacturing activity.

RALSWIEK

Around the middle of the eighth century, merchants established a port settlement at Ralswiek, on the island of Rügen in the Baltic Sea, off the northeastern coast of Germany. This commercial center, with settlement, shipping facilities, cemetery, and cult site, thrived for some five centuries before being replaced by new port cities of the Hanseatic League.

Houses on the settlement were sturdily built with planks and nails. The urban community was supported by cereal and vegetable crops grown in the agricultural lands inland from the port, and it was supplied with meat from cattle, pigs, and sheep. As we would expect at such a location, these farm products were supplemented by fish. Workshops at Ralswiek were engaged in iron smithing; copper and bronze working; carving of bone, antler, and horn; comb manufacturing; and glass bead making. Trade based at the site was local and long distance. Local trade brought farm products and raw materials into the port city. Long-distance trade brought raw materials such as stone for whetstones from Norway and the Rhineland, and finished goods fashioned in other parts of Europe, such as soapstone bowls, fine pottery, and jewelry.

A hoard of 2,211 silver coins found at Ralswiek brings home the extraordinary wealth and the long-distance interactions in which the community was engaged. The hoard was buried sometime in the first half of the ninth century, and the coins in it were mostly from central Asia and the Middle East. Like many other trade centers of northern Europe during these centuries, Ralswiek played a vital role in commerce that linked western Europe and southwest Asia.

STARAJA LADOGA

In the northeasternmost region of Europe, a trade center that developed into a town was established during the seventh century at Ladoga, on the Volkhov River in northwestern Russia.

As at other production and commercial centers discussed, here too metalworking is abundantly evident, including the processing of gold and silver, metals that were used exclusively for making ornaments and for storing wealth. Debris from manufacturing shows that bone and antler were carved on the settlement. Ships were built and repaired here.

Most significantly, the commercial town at Ladoga provided a major link in the trade networks that connected western Europe, the north, and Byzantium and Arabia to the east. Trade routes that extended from Ladoga south and east along the rivers of Russia to the Black Sea carried silver coins from the Arab lands, coins from Byzantium, and beads made from rock crystal and carnelian in the eastern Mediterranean, as well as other kinds of eastern jewelry. From the west came combs fashioned from bone and antler and ornamental glass beads.

After Ladoga had thrived as a trade center linking west, north, and east for a century or so, a new commercial town was established farther upstream on the Volkhov River. This town became the major medieval metropolis of Novgorod.

HAITHABU/HEDEBY

During the seventh century, a new town was established at the base of the peninsula of Jutland at a point where goods could be transshipped a distance of only six miles. This saved ships the long and dangerous journey northward around Jutland carrying cargoes of goods between the trade centers of the Baltic and regions to the east, such as Ladoga, and the commercial towns of the west, such as Dorestad. Haithabu (Danish Hedeby) was a wholly new town, established where there had been no substantial population before and founded expressly as a transshipment place between western and eastern towns and markets. Here, too, archaeologists have recovered remains of extensive iron production, bone and antler working, pottery manufacturing, glass bead making, and textile weaving. The evidence for trade is extensive.

From northern Europe came amber, furs, honey, soapstone vessels, and beeswax. From the Rhineland to the south and west came glassware, grindstones hewn from basalt, ornate metal jewelry, pottery, and wine. Textiles came from the lands around the mouth of the Rhine. A mint began producing coins at Haithabu, so important was the commercial function of this place. During the ninth and tenth centuries, Haithabu was one of the largest towns north of the Alps, rivaling in size and economic activity major old Roman cities such as Cologne.

By the ninth century, the time at which the changes brought by Charlemagne were having wide repercussions throughout Europe, the northern coasts of Europe were dotted with thriving towns and cities. In addition to those mentioned in chapter 5 were Dorestad, in the Netherlands; Southampton, Ipswich, and York, in England; Dublin, in Ireland; Kaupang and Bergen, in Norway; Birka, Åhus, and Uppåkra, in Sweden; Ribe, in Denmark; Haithabu/Hedeby and Ralswiek, in Germany; Grobin, in Latvia; and Ladoga, in Russia. A new form of urban center, different in many respects from that of the Roman world, had emerged in northern Europe. These new urban centers could grow and prosper because of great technological advances that were being made in the countryside where food and supplies (such as hides, leather, textiles, bone, antler, and timber) that were needed by the expanding towns and cities were produced.

8
The Revolution in the Countryside

❖

IN A TEXT WRITTEN AROUND A.D. 1000, A FARMER described his daily routine this way.

> I work very hard; I go out at daybreak, drive the oxen to the field and yoke them to the plow. Never is winter weather so severe that I . . . remain at home . . . But when the oxen are yoked to the plow and the share and coulter are fastened on, every day I must plow a full acre or more.

This brief description of the farmer's task may sound like terrible drudgery to us, but it represents a revolution in agricultural technology that took place during the Dark Ages. This revolution greatly improved the nutrition of Europeans and made possible a host of advances in manufacturing, trade, and the arts. Because food is a basic need, the production of enough food to feed the population must be the first priority of every society. When farming techniques improve in efficiency, fewer people are needed to produce food, so more people can devote their energies to other tasks. The revolution in plowing technology was the basis for all of the great economic, social, and cultural developments of the Middle Ages.

The plow that was in general use in the Roman world was a simple scratch plow, known as an *ard*. It was a pointed piece of wood that was dragged through the top layer of soil, making a narrow ditch, or furrow, in which the farmer sowed seeds. During the fifth and sixth centuries, a whole new kind of plow was developed by local engineers working to create a more efficient machine. This was the moldboard plow, which included a series of new technical elements and permitted the farmer to work heavier and more productive soils than was possible with the earlier tools. The new plow had an iron coulter, shaped like a knife, that sliced through the topsoil; a metal-tipped share that cut underneath the earth that had been sliced by the coulter; and a moldboard, mounted obliquely behind the share, that turned over the chunks of earth as the plow moved along. The most complex plows had a pair of wheels in front of the coulter to ease the passage of the machine across the field. This new device meant that farmers could produce crops much more efficiently by plowing more quickly than had been possible before, by turning the soil rather than simply opening a small furrow and thus moving the nutrients from below into the upper layers, and by making accessible rich, heavy loams that could not be worked easily with the simple scratch plows.

Other technological improvements also contributed to making food production more efficient. The development of the

Figure 8.1. Reconstruction of the farming village at Vorbasse, in Denmark, showing what it may have looked like in the eighth century. Note the long houses, the smaller buildings, and the fenced divisions between different farmsteads in the settlement.

horse collar allowed this faster and stronger animal to replace oxen on some farms as the draft animals pulling the plow. The introduction of the three-field system increased agricultural yields. One set of fields was planted with winter cereals—wheat, barley, or rye. One was planted with peas or beans, or sometimes with oats and alfalfa as feed for horses. The third was left fallow. Livestock could graze on the fallow fields, manuring them for planting in the next season.

These three changes—the moldboard plow, the horse collar, and the three-field system—enabled farmers to feed their communities at an unprecedented level of efficiency. The new technologies were introduced at different times in different parts of Europe, but everywhere their impact was revolutionary.

LIFE IN THE COUNTRYSIDE

We can learn the most about what life was like for people who lived in the countryside by looking at the results of the archaeological studies of their villages. For examples here, I examine two villages—one that was within the former boundaries of the Roman Empire and one that was outside of them.

Brebières was a typical settlement of late sixth-century northern Gaul, now in France, situated on fertile and well-watered soils three miles south-southeast of the city of Douai, near the border with Belgium. Archaeologists who excavated the settlement found the remains of thirty small rectangular structures, their walls supported by vertical posts, the bottoms of which had been sunk into holes dug in the ground. Pottery, iron implements, and stone tools were among the most abundant materials associated with the dwellings. Fragmentary bronze ornaments such as brooches were found in some of the houses, as were fragments of glass vessels. Among bone implements, combs were relatively common.

At this typical rural settlement of the sixth century, the houses were small and plain. There is no trace of any larger architecture, such as a leader's house, a public assembly hall, or a ritual structure such as a chapel. But material culture is abundant and of good quality. Much of the pottery is decorated. Iron was readily available and was used to make a wide range of implements, including nails, belt buckles, and knives. Bronze was not common, but a number of personal ornaments of this valuable metal show that bronze was available and people in this community had something they could trade for it. The copper and tin that constitute bronze had to be mined elsewhere in Europe, then smelted and brought together to make the bronze alloy.

Spindle whorls show that people were spinning fibers to make textiles. Bone combs indicate that members of the community were making these important objects or trading valued goods for them. Like bronze, the fragments of ornate glass vessels show that the community had important outside contacts and had wealth to trade for imported luxury goods. Glass beads at the site were less costly than vessels but still required a technology to produce that was probably not practiced at Brebières. They, too, represent trade goods imported from elsewhere.

The archaeological evidence at Brebières shows that a typical community of this period lived a rather modest life compared to modern Western standards or the lifestyles of elites of the Roman provinces. But the people had ready access to iron, which they put to use for a variety of purposes. They took the trouble to decorate their pottery even though plain vessels would have contained food and drink just as well. And they were able to import into their little community a variety of desired goods from outside—bronze ornaments and decorative glass beads that they wore on their persons, and ornate glass vessels that must have been used to hold beverages on special occasions.

Study of nearly four thousand fragmentary animal bones from the site indicate a great preponderance of domestic animals (about 96 percent) forming the basis of the meat protein part of the diet. These were mainly cattle, pigs, sheep, and goats. In much smaller quantities are bones of wild animals, especially red deer and boar. Domesticated chicken and other fowl are represented, along with wild birds.

Although the members of this typical farming village lived modest lives by modern standards, their diet was diverse, and there is no evidence that their lives were unusually harsh. They also had access to a wide range of craft technologies to produce objects they needed, as well as the ability to acquire luxury goods through trade with other communities.

Well beyond the frontiers of the Roman Empire, on the Jutland peninsula of Denmark, the village of Vorbasse was inhabited continuously from the first to the eleventh century. Comparison of the settlements on the site during the late Roman period and early medieval times (the eighth and ninth centuries) highlights the changes that took place in the intervening years. In the earlier period, the settlement consisted of thirteen farmsteads, each within a fenced enclosure roughly fifty-five by fifty-five yards in size (slightly more than half an acre). Ten of the enclosures were arranged in two parallel rows with an open space between them; the other three enclosures were just north of them. In the middle of each enclosure was a longhouse built with vertical posts sunk into the ground that supported wattle-and-daub walls and a thatched roof. Each longhouse was divided into sections, one for human habitation and one for livestock. Also in the enclosures were one or two small houses, a couple of bins for storing grain, and a workshop. Millstones for grinding grain were in the houses; furnaces for processing iron were situated outside the settlement. Wells, dug in low areas of the site, were lined with wickerwork. Wooden ladders were found in some wells. If a typical family inhabiting one of the longhouses was made up of eight to ten persons, and the one or two smaller buildings housed an average of five or six persons who were economically dependent upon the landowner in the big house, the total population of Vorbasse in this period may have been between 200 and 250 people.

By the eighth century, changes in the layout of the settlement indicate a growth in population and important changes in the scale and intensity of economic activity in this village. The houses (the longhouses and the smaller structures) were built much more sturdily, with massive roof-bearing posts at the two ends. The settlement at this time consisted of seven farmsteads in two groups on either side of a road—three farmsteads to the south, four to the north. The longhouses were much larger in area, usually more than a hundred feet in length, and all had stalls to accommodate between twenty and thirty cattle. The enclosures were about four times as large as those of the earlier period—about two acres in size. In many enclosures, rows of small houses were packed tightly together along the interior sides of the fences. The population of the village in this phase may have been between four hundred and five hundred people. All of the farmstead enclosures had gates that opened onto the road; between the longhouses and the gates were often many small workshops. Many more workshops were in use in this period, and they were often substantially larger than those of the earlier settlement.

The large houses were the residences of well-to-do and socially prominent farmers; the smaller houses were dwellings of tenant farmers and crafts workers. The changes that took place between the earlier settlement and the later one show that the more powerful farmers had gained considerably in material wealth and were able to maintain much larger numbers of farmworkers and crafts workers. Each farmstead had become more productive, and the enclosed areas were much larger. The larger number and sizes of workshops indicate a greater role for manufacturing. The situation of the workshops near the gates leading to the road suggests that much of this production was for export. The succession of villages at Vorbasse shows substantial economic and demographic growth in a rural community that lay outside of the former Roman provinces.

FOOD PRODUCTION AND DIET

With the ending of Roman taxation and commercial systems, communities could become more autonomous and self-sufficient than they had been under Roman political domination. That is not to say that every community became independent—far from it. Ties between communities were still important. Even though villagers no longer had to pay taxes to the Roman government, they still had to support the elites who had assumed the roles of political leaders, whether chiefs or kings or whatever designation might be appropriate in the varying circumstances.

Farmers grew wheat, barley, oats, and rye as their main crops, and they used these cereals to make bread, porridge, and beer. Vegetable crops included peas, lentils, beans, cabbage, turnips, beets, carrots, and celery. Dill and coriander were grown. Apples, pears, and plums were cultivated, as were walnuts. Peaches and apricots were grown west of the Rhine. Strawberries, raspberries, elderberries, cherries, and hazelnuts were gathered in the summer and fall months.

The principal livestock was cattle, but the farmers also raised pigs, sheep, and goats for food and other products, including milk, leather, wool, and traction power. Chickens, ducks, and geese were also raised for food. Horses and donkeys and even dogs were eaten on occasion.

Communities brewed their own beer and mead and made

cider. Wine was imported from the Mediterranean world, to be consumed by elites. Well-to-do persons also had access to a variety of other imported foods, many of which had also been available during Roman times, including olive oil, figs, dates, almonds, and spices such as coriander and caraway.

The typical meal was prepared by putting vegetables, cereals, and sometimes small amounts of meat into a stewpot over a fire. Grains could be ground into flour to make bread as well as eaten in the form of porridge or gruel. Aside from fruit, honey was the principal source of sweetness. Most people shared their meals with their families or fellows, all eating from a common bowl. Elites had access to individual bowls and cups, and they were frequently able to enhance their meals with olive oil and spices. Some elites also had access to special cuts of meat for roasting rather than just the small chunks of meat for stewing that most people ate. The importance of this social distinction in meat consumption is emphasized by the presence of iron roasting spits in many richly outfitted graves.

Besides food, the farming villages produced a variety of materials that their inhabitants needed and wanted. Each family made its own clothing from wool and from linen, for which flax was cultivated in the fields. A part-time potter made the bowls, dishes, and cups needed by all of the villagers. Probably one smith in each village worked with an assistant to smelt local iron ore to make metal, then forged the metal into tools such as knives, shovels, axes, plowshares, and scythes. In the evenings, especially in winter when outdoor work was limited by darkness and cold, people made tools from wood, bone, and antler. To obtain goods that were not locally available, such as glass beads and bronze for ornamental fittings, the community produced surplus goods for exchange, such as salted meat, cheese, leather, and perhaps finished textiles, iron tools, and items carved from bone and antler.

NUTRITION AND STATURE

Skeletal remains in the cemeteries tell us much about how well people were fed and how tall they were. Stature is often a good indication of the overall health of a population. A recent large-scale analysis of bones from the Anglo-Saxon cemetery at Berinsfield, in Oxfordshire, England, has been especially informative. Chemical analyses of samples from bones of many individuals in the cemetery indicate that substantial amounts of animal protein were eaten consistently—a key indicator of nutritional quality. Some persons ate more protein than others, but no one was deprived of this important source of nutrition. There seem to have been no major differences in overall nutrition according to social status, though the bones indicate some minor differences in the quality but not quantity of what different individuals ate. These results of analyses from Britain are consistent with findings from cemeteries on the continent. It must be noted, however, that studies of skeletal remains and nutrition at different cemeteries have yielded somewhat varying results, underscoring the high degree of local variability in dietary practices.

Measurements taken on skeletal remains in cemeteries in southwestern Germany indicate that the average height for men was about five feet eight inches, for women about five feet four inches, statures well above those of late medieval and early modern times. Measurements taken on skeletons in other regions are comparable. In Denmark, for example, the average height for men was about five feet nine inches—

just above those for southwestern Germany—and for women about five feet four inches. These average heights were not achieved again until the twentieth century. Compared with earlier and later populations in the same regions, these average measurements show that most people had adequate nutrition during most of their lives and their living conditions were generally good.

REGULATING COMMUNITIES: THE LAW

Just as communities throughout Europe were linked together through trade (chapter 10), they were also connected by systems of laws that regulated interpersonal behavior. After the decline of Roman power and influence, the emerging nations—the Franks, the Anglo-Saxons, and others—established formalized and written legal codes of their own. These codes were based in part on each group's own traditions and in part on the Roman law that had been in effect during the time of the Empire. The law codes of the different post-Roman peoples of Europe had many features in common, but each legal system also had its own special emphases. The codes of the different Germanic groups were written first in Latin, that of the Anglo-Saxons in Old English. Among early examples are the Code of Euric—the laws of the Visigoths first compiled in 471—and the *Pactus Alamannorum,* the code of the Alamanni, written around 500.

The first formal and written law code of the Franks, the *Pactus Legis Salicae,* dates from about A.D. 510. The earliest law code of which we have evidence among the Anglo-Saxons was written around the year 598. Both of these legal codes emphasize issues that especially concerned the agricultural populations of rural areas, such as land disputes. Much attention was paid in these codes to penalty payments that had to be made if one person injured another.

Thus quite quickly after the end of Roman power, the newly emerging peoples were already creating codified legal systems to regulate interactions between individuals and communities. These legal systems provided the social and political mechanisms that enabled the revolution that was brought about by the new plow technology to expand into the realms of manufacturing and commerce, as discussed in the next two chapters.

9
Crafting Tools and Ornaments for the New Societies

❖

AT THE AGE OF TWELVE IN THE YEAR 601, ELIGIUS was apprenticed to a goldsmith named Abbo. The boy, son of farmers near Limoges, in France, was described as combining in his person "the innocence of the dove with the cleverness of the snake." He learned his craft well and gained important commissions from the Frankish royal family. In later life, he was described this way:

> Eligius was of strong build and had a healthy color, fine curly hair, delicate hands, and narrow fingers. His bearing was of honesty and intelligence. He wore gold and precious stones on his clothing. He had a gold belt and gold decorated purses, richly embroidered shirts, and coats bordered with gold. All his clothes were very costly, many of silk.

We do not know the names of most of the men and women who worked at crafts and industry in Europe during the period of our concern. Yet many of the objects they made are available for study, excavated from settlements and cemeteries, in church treasuries, or in museums. This material evidence reveals a great deal about what people manufactured, where, and how. Eligius is highly unusual in that we know something about his life story as well as his craft. Most crafts workers did not make gold ornaments for kings and become wealthy, as Eligius did, but, as we learn from the objects with which a few crafts specialists were buried, others did acquire some wealth and status through their labors.

For a picture of more characteristic manufacturing activity, we turn to material evidence that can show how and where things were made. The principal products fall into two categories—tools and ornaments. The new objects in both categories played important roles in economic and social developments during the fifth through eighth centuries.

HELGÖ AND OTHER NEW CENTERS

On the small island of Lillon in Lake Mälaren, eighteen miles west of Stockholm, in central Sweden, lie the physical remains of a remarkable manufacturing and commercial center. Here, seven hundred miles north of the Roman Empire, an industrial community of intercontinental importance thrived from the middle of the third until the eighth century. The workshops at Helgö turned out large quantities of iron tools and weapons, bronze jewelry, gold ornaments, and other products. The scale of industrial activity at this small island settlement is extraordinary. Among the iron tools made and used at

Helgö were hammers, files, borers, chisels, and locks and keys. Arrowheads were forged. Archaeologists have recovered some ten thousand pieces of ceramic molds used for casting bronze jewelry, and several hundred pounds of fragments of crucibles, the containers in which metals were melted for pouring into molds. The workshops at Helgö were producing many of the principal types of fibulae (brooches) that were in use in Europe during the fifth and sixth centuries. Fine jewelers' tools for working gold and silver include hammers, files, scrapers, gravers, chasing implements, tongs, and scribers. Glass beads of different colors and designs were crafted. Much of the ornamental material manufactured at Helgö was of forms common throughout Europe, indicating that this production center was closely linked to the circulation systems that connected communities throughout the continent.

Although much of the industrial produce of the Helgö workshops was destined for consumers in Sweden and neighboring parts of the Baltic Sea region, objects imported from far away that have been found at Helgö attest to the community's links with distant lands (chapter 10). A bronze Buddha figure made in India in the sixth century was recovered at Helgö, as were bronze basins and coins from continental Europe and bishop's crozier from Ireland.

The abundant evidence at Helgö for the processing of iron to make tools and weapons, bronze for personal ornaments, glass for beads, antler and bone to make combs and pins, and amber for beads and amulets is replicated at other manufacturing centers throughout temperate Europe between the fifth and eighth centuries. Many of these places are on the coasts of northern Europe. Coastal manufacturing sites include Helgö's successor, Birka, in central Sweden; Lundeborg, in central Denmark; Ribe, on Denmark's west coast; Hamwic/

Southampton, in southern England; Dinas Powys, in southern Wales; Dorestad, near the mouth of the Rhine; and Haithabu/Hedeby, in southeastern Jutland. Inland sites include Klein Köris, in northeastern Germany, and the Runder Berg, in southwestern Germany. When we compare the objects made at these sites and the industrial debris in the workshops, it is striking how similar the manufacturing industries were at these commercial centers all over Europe.

The Runder Berg is an example of such a manufacturing center in the middle of the continent. The site is the most thoroughly investigated of about fifty hilltop settlements in this part of Europe dating from the fourth to the sixth century. As at the sites on the coasts of the North Sea, Irish Sea, and Baltic Sea, crafts workers at the Runder Berg employed a range of different materials. They forged iron weapons and tools. Hammers, anvils, tongs, punches, and chisels show the variety of smithing implements they used. Bronze, much of it obtained from melting down old Roman vessels and reused belt attachments, was recast into new ornaments. Models, partly finished objects, and molds recovered at the Runder Berg show that ornate fibulae and belt buckles were among the special personal paraphernalia fashioned there. Silver and gold work attest to the specialized manufacture of precious ornaments for elites. Glass was being shaped into vessels and beads. Antler, bone, jet, and lead were among other materials that these crafts workers fashioned into tools and ornaments.

MOBILE MANUFACTURERS

Although commodities such as iron tools, glass beads, and antler combs were manufactured in large quantities at specific places, such as Helgö and the Runder Berg, many items, such as ornamental jewelry, were made by mobile crafts workers—metalworkers who traveled through the landscape making objects for customers on demand. The metalworkers carried with them their fine implements for crafting gold and silver jewelry, and they were sometimes buried with the tools of their trade. Those tools included delicate hammers and small iron anvils, scales and weights, and bronze models for fibulae that would be cast in silver or gold. Two smith's graves, one from Austria and one from Hungary, are particularly informative.

A grave in the small cemetery at Poysdorf, in Lower Austria, contained the skeleton of a man who was laid to rest sometime around A.D. 535. Placed with his body were objects that mark his status as an elite male in his community, along with a whole series of objects that attest to his role as a metalsmith. A short sword, parts of a shield, and iron belt attachments are characteristic of men identified as warriors. (The grave had been robbed; it is possible that additional weapons were present originally.) Items of personal grooming included bronze tweezers and a comb made from antler. Next to his right leg were tools for forging iron and casting bronze. Corroded remains of a lock are probably from a wooden box that had contained the implements. The tools included an anvil, three hammers of different sizes, two pairs of tongs, a file, a whetstone, a burin made of bone, and a black spherical stone. The stone had minute particles of silver on it, indicating that it had been used to polish silver objects. Also present were two bronze models of fibulae, the final versions of which were to be of silver.

The combination of weapons and smithing tools in the grave indicates that this man had been a warrior and a specialized craftsman. As a smith, he made iron tools and cast silver jewelry. It is significant that all of this man's crafts-working equipment was compact enough to be easily carried. Clearly, such a craftsman did not need to be tied to a workshop but could travel, making objects for customers in different places.

A similar conclusion emerges from a grave in a small cemetery at Kunszentmárton, in Hungary, but here we see something more. This man was buried, around 610, with weapons and horse harness gear as well as tools and models for making metal ornaments. In this case, the ornaments were not fibulae but sheet metal relief objects that could be made of gold, silver, or bronze. These ornaments were for decorating horse harness equipment, belt attachments, or sword scabbards. The striking thing about them is that they represent styles that are associated with different regional traditions. If any one of these was found alone in the grave, the man would be linked to the stylistic tradition of the region in which that style was common. These models representing different regional traditions show that this craftsman could make ornaments suiting the fashions of several different groups of people. Apparently, he crafted objects according to the tastes of his customers rather than his own home tradition.

THE PRODUCTS

What was the purpose of the different industries? For iron tools, pottery, and textiles, the answer seems straightforward: People needed these things for the basic tasks of everyday life—to chop down trees and build houses, cut meat, prepare meals, and make clothes. But what about brooches, pendants, glass beads, and other ornaments? Why did people need these? Four examples—pottery, swords, fibulae, and combs—illuminate the character of some of these craft industries.

Pottery is the most abundant category of archaeological material during the first millennium, and from pottery we can learn a great deal about social and economic changes. Pottery was essential for cooking, serving, and storing food and beverages. Everyone used pottery, though the character of pottery used by different people in society was different. Elite individuals had access to finer and more highly decorated wares. Pottery vessels are fragile and break when dropped, but sherds of well-fired pottery survive in the ground indefinitely. It is one of the most informative sources we have for understanding changes in people's lives.

During the post-Roman period, most pottery in the formerly Roman imperial lands was made on the potter's wheel. In some cases, these industries continued to produce pottery similar to the Roman types that had been in special favor. In the Argonne region of northeastern France, for example, pottery similar to Roman terra sigillata was made. At Mayen, in the middle Rhineland, the pottery industry established during Roman times was carried on straight through post-Roman times and into the High Middle Ages. North of Mayen, between the cities of Bonn and Cologne, on rich deposits of fine clay along the west side of the Rhine River, pottery industries were established during the seventh century that continued to provide fine ceramics for much of northern Europe throughout the Middle Ages. Large numbers of kilns and of pits containing fragments of misfired pottery attest to the scale of the manufacturing in the villages of Badorf and Pingsdorf. Great quantities of these ceramics in settlements throughout the Rhineland, northern continental Europe, southern Britain, and even Scandinavia show how far these fine wares were traded.

Swords were available only to elite males in society and were the principal symbol of their special status. Swords were not crafted in most communities but only by specialized smiths. Most were made by complex processes of packet welding or damascening, which could be performed only by highly trained and skilled specialists. In northern France from the fifth century, there is good evidence for the existence of specialized workshops that produced the long iron swords that were the favored weapon of the elite. Highly ornate swords and scabbards were trimmed with gold inset with sparkling red garnets, and in the sixth century some long iron swords were outfitted with gold-plated hilts (see Figure 4.3). Plain iron swords with scabbards made of iron or wood greatly outnumbered these lavishly decorated weapons.

Fibulae, or brooches, were made of bronze, iron, silver, gold, or a combination of these metals. They served to fasten clothing together, but they also had important decorative functions. In contrast to fibulae of the Roman period, those of early medieval times often had broad, flat surfaces that bore complex ornament. Like all jewelry, fibulae were designed to be seen and have specific effects on the observer. They were worn in places on the body where they were highly visible—on the chest or on the front of the shoulder. Studies by cognitive psychologists have shown that the ornamental patterns and motifs that jewelers created on Dark Age fibulae were designed especially to grab and hold the viewer's attention. The technique of chip-carving (see chapter 3) produced many facets that reflected the light, creating a mesmerizing sparkling effect. Many fibulae bear complex curvilinear patterns, like mazes, that draw the attention of the viewer. Especially characteristic of fibulae of this period is stylized animal ornament, another device that was intended to attract and hold the attention of a person looking at the object. Unlike images of animals applied to personal ornaments during the Roman period, animals were

Figure 9.1. Drawing of a gilded bronze fibula, from Chessel Down in southern England (length $5^{1/3}$ inches). The human faces, animal heads and legs, and relief ornament are visible on the head (top) and foot (bottom) of this brooch.

no longer portrayed naturalistically. Now the creatures were stylized, with features of one kind of animal often blending into features of another.

Fibulae were devices used to communicate information about status and identity. They ranged from small and simple pins made of bronze or iron (the most common) to large silver or gold ornaments inset with garnets (restricted to the wealthy and powerful). Besides status, fibulae conveyed information about regional identity. As the new kingdoms formed during the fifth, sixth, and seventh centuries, different peoples developed distinctive varieties of fibulae. Frankish fibulae are different from Alamannic fibulae; Anglo-Saxon are different from Gothic. Whereas today we mark regional identity with national and state flags, or baseball caps with our home team's insignia, in early medieval Europe fibulae told who you were.

For most of us, combs are cheap plastic implements that we use once or twice a day and do not think much about. But they meant something very different to people fifteen hundred years ago. Combs were common objects in burials, especially in the more richly outfitted graves. They were most often made of red deer antler or cattle bone, less frequently of wood, iron, or bronze, and often they were ornamented with incised patterns, lines or dots, and sometimes representations of animals. On an important carved stone found at Niederdollendorf, on the Rhine, one side bears a representation believed to be the earliest picture of Christ in the Rhineland (dating to the sixth century). On the other side is an image of a warrior, with sword and canteen, shown combing his hair.

Combs were made at manufacturing centers all over Europe, including those mentioned at the beginning of this chapter. Estimates suggest that a comb represents about fifty hours of work. The process involved sawing red deer antler into cylinders of appropriate length, splitting the cylinders of antler into several segments, carving these pieces, sawing the shape of the teeth, then assembling the complete object from the separately crafted parts. Comb making was a craft done by specialists, not by every household. Distribution evidence shows that a specialist may have served a region about ten miles in diameter. Burial evidence shows that combs were used by women and men, but only individuals of special status were buried with combs.

Why were combs so important? Many peoples attributed magical properties to hair, which plays an important role in folklore and mythology (think of the story of Rapunzel and her golden hair). Hair can be a signaling device, used in the same ways that clothing and jewelry are, to communicate information about individuals—the group to which they belong, their status, and so forth. Special knots have been identified in the hair of many of the bodies found preserved in the bogs of northern Europe. The Roman historian Tacitus, writing around A.D. 100, mentions such knots in his descriptions of some of the peoples he includes in his work *Germania*. Hair is also linked to themes of life force and eternal life, perhaps because hair continues to grow long after the body itself has reached its maximum size.

Between A.D. 400 and 800, new craft industries expanded to include a variety of different materials. Some were products of direct economic importance, such as the pottery needed for everyday meal preparation, and swords required for defending or capturing property. Other crafts produced objects that were used to express people's changing identities as the new societies grew in power and into Europe-wide importance. As the manufacturing systems expanded, so did the commercial networks through which the goods flowed.

10

Royal Exchange and Everyday Trade

❖

IN THE YEAR 796, CHARLEMAGNE, SELF-DESCRIBED "King of the Franks and Lombards and Patrician of Rome," sent a letter to Offa, king of Mercia, in the central part of England, about matters of trade.

> It is our will and command that [merchants] have full protection in our kingdom to transact their lawful business according to ancient practice. If they are anywhere unjustly treated, they should appeal to us or to our judges and we will then see that justice is done.

The same letter speaks of gifts that Charlemagne has sent to Offa.

> I have sent you . . . a belt and a Hunnish sword and two silk cloaks. . . .

From these words, written for Charlemagne by his chamberlain, Alcuin, we learn two important facts about trade in the eighth century. First, merchants traveled, apparently freely, in Charlemagne's kingdom, and they had the protection and approval of the king. Royal encouragement of "free trade" was certainly a great advantage to commercial entrepreneurs. Second, Charlemagne (and presumably Offa and other kings of the time) practiced royal gift exchange. Charlemagne mentions three items of special status and value that he is sending to his counterpart king across the Channel.

Trade expanded rapidly during the fifth, sixth, seventh, and eighth centuries, but we rarely have texts such as this one by Charlemagne that explain how trade worked. Trade was an everyday affair and not of major concern to church officials, who were the principal sources of written information about this period. But the archaeological evidence for trade is abundant and rich in information.

TINTAGEL AND DORESTAD

On the windswept rock promontory of Tintagel, on the coast of Cornwall in the west of England, archaeologists have recovered masses of luxury imports from Spain, northern Africa, and the eastern end of the Mediterranean Sea. These include large ceramic amphoras for transporting wine and olive oil, finely crafted bowls and plates, and ornate glass beakers—all elegant tableware that wealthy rulers used to host feasts and banquets. These luxury objects arrived throughout the fifth, sixth, and seventh centuries. Why would this weather-beaten rock on the northwestern edge of the Eurasian landmass be the site of importation for some of the most lavish and highly desired products of the Mediterranean world?

Figure 10.1. Tintagel, on the coast of Cornwall, western England. The path leads from the mainland on the right across the narrow bridge to the rocky mass that housed a small but politically and commercially important community during the fifth and sixth centuries.

The rock of Tintagel, 27 acres in area and rising an average of 190 feet above the surrounding sea, is connected to the mainland by a narrow and treacherous ridge that is almost eroded away. Tintagel looks like an island, and as the erosion progresses it will be one soon. The entire perimeter is steep sided, making access from below extremely difficult. On the mainland side of the rocky ridge is a huge ditch that was dug in the sixth century as further protection for the community on Tintagel. A small sandy beach on the promotory's north side offered the only possible harbor for ships bearing cargo. Despite these extraordinarily difficult circumstances, the site of Tintagel has yielded more fine pottery from Mediterranean workshops than all other sites in the British Isles combined. Only about 5 percent of the site has been excavated; more surprises surely await us.

Near the mouth of the Rhine River in the Netherlands, at what is today the town of Wijk bij Duurstede (Dorestad), farmers had long been digging animal bones out of their fields and grinding them up to make glue and bonemeal fertilizer. In the middle of the nineteenth century, it came to the attention of officials that large quantities of cultural material—iron tools and pottery, as well as the bone remains of meals—were being found in the fields. Systematic excavations in the twentieth century revealed the layout of a major port, with extensive docks, houses of merchant traders, and vast quantities of trade goods as well as the remains of everyday life represented by the animal bones. Dates obtained from tree rings on oak slats from barrels that had been sunk into the ground to line wells show that the trading settlement began to grow in the seventh century. Large amounts of pottery, iron tools, and coins indicate that this place was the site of a highly active trading center during the eighth and ninth centuries. Other materials that attest to the port's role in interregional commerce include grindstones of basalt, stone weights, whetstones, bronze ornaments, glass vessels, and glass beads. In fact, historical sources tell us that Dorestad was the principal port for Charlemagne's empire. Through Dorestad, merchants brought goods from elsewhere on the coasts of the Atlantic, North Sea, and Baltic Sea into the European heartland, and they shipped materials from the Rhineland to northern France, Britain, and Scandinavia. Dorestad played the role that Rotterdam in the Netherlands (the world's busiest port) plays today—the transit site for goods circulating between the heart of Europe and the rest of the world.

CENTERS AND NETWORKS

These two places—the windswept rock on the northwestern fringes of the European continent and the riverine port that served as the principal commercial link between Charlemagne's empire and the outside world—exemplify the extremes of commercial centers in temperate Europe during these centuries. Many such commercial centers of interregional scope flourished between the fifth and eighth centuries; these are discussed in chapters 5, 6, and 7. All these centers are situated on or close to the seacoasts of northern Europe. Before the Industrial Revolution, moving goods by water was vastly cheaper than moving them overland. Estimates suggest that a given quantity of goods costs twenty-five times as much to send by land as by sea. To and from these coastal centers, ships carried bulk commodities such as wheat, amphoras of wine, and finely crafted luxury goods such as silver bowls and gold jewelry.

Almost all of the evidence we have for bulk transport comes from seaports. But trade was not limited to these coastal centers. They were parts of complex networks of communities throughout Europe along which all types of goods circulated. Every settlement and cemetery that is studied archaeologically gives us evidence for the circulation of goods, including bronze fibulae, amber beads, and imported pottery. Such evidence tells us not only that objects were being moved from place to place but also that people were moving—whether for purposes of trade, pilgrimage, visiting family, plunder, or missionizing—and were bringing things with them. Whenever things are transported, ideas and information move as well.

Many different mechanisms of exchange were involved in the circulation of goods. Barter trade—the exchange of goods of equal value—was important. Gift-giving played a major role as well; family members gave presents to one another, and rulers practiced diplomatic exchanges, as in the example of gift exchange between Charlemagne and Offa cited at the beginning of this chapter. People gave gifts to gods and spirits, depositing them at churches or at traditional sanctuaries, anticipating favors in return. In many situations, farmers made tribute payments in goods to their local chiefs or kings; these were forms of rent or taxes in economies in which not everyone used coined money. Plunder during raids also resulted in goods being moved from one community to another.

ROUTES AND VEHICLES

By late prehistoric times, Europe was honeycombed with pathways across fields, through forests, over mountain passes, and even through swamps where wooden trackways were built to permit dry passage. During this period, travelers used these routes intensively. Many of the roads that the Roman army constructed followed these natural routes through the landscape, and post-Roman travelers often found themselves trudging along the remains of the Roman road system. Rivers were much used for travel and trade; they included the small tributaries as well as the great rivers of Europe, such as the Rhine, the Danube, the Rhône, the Elbe, and the Thames. Commerce across the English Channel and the North and Baltic seas was also intensive.

For overland transport, various kinds of vehicles were used, depending upon the character and quantity of the goods and the nature of the terrain. Individual merchants and traveling crafts workers walked, carrying their wares in packs on their backs. Wagons pulled by horses or oxen were used to transport bulk goods, but they were effective only in relatively flat landscapes and during dry weather conditions. Pack animals were more versatile. They could be loaded with goods and could traverse much more rugged terrain than wagons could.

On rivers, different kinds of boats and rafts were employed, depending upon the quantities of goods to be moved, the distance, and the size of the body of water. On the high seas, much more complex and specialized craft were needed to cope with waves, tides, storms, and distance. From earlier periods, a wide range of dugout canoes and timber-frame boats have been found, preserved in the mud of bogs and river bottoms. From the period in question, fewer boats have survived; the best preserved are oceangoing warships rather than freighters. But the nautical technology that went into building these boats gives us a good idea about what ships used for trade were like.

The Nydam boat was excavated in a bog deposit in what is now northern Germany, near the city of Schleswig. It was made of oak planks ("clinker-built") and was about seventy-seven feet long and thirteen feet wide at the widest part. The ship was designed to be powered by thirty rowers. Dendrochronological analysis (tree-ring dating) of the wood used in its construction indicates that it was built between A.D. 310 and 320.

The ship excavated in the rich burial at Sutton Hoo, in East Anglia in southeastern England, was built around A.D. 600. Like the Nydam boat, this was also made of oak planks, but it differed from the earlier vessel in having iron bolts and nails attaching the frame to the hull. The Sutton Hoo ship was eighty-nine feet long and fourteen feet wide at the broadest and was powered by forty rowers working the oars.

Neither of these well-documented ships had any trace of a mast. Sails were used in the Mediterranean world in Roman times and earlier, but the first use of sails in northern Europe is evidenced in pictures carved on standing stones on the Swedish island of Gotland, dating to the seventh century. Both the Nydam and the Sutton Hoo boats were strongly built, seaworthy craft, and they could certainly have been used to transport trade goods across the North Sea, the Baltic Sea, the English Channel, and the Irish Sea. But the boats that were employed in bulk trade were probably designed differently, with more space available for storing goods and less to accommodate the large numbers of rowers.

OBJECTS IN CIRCULATION

A few examples illustrate the complex patterns in the movement of goods.

Basalt lava quarried at Mayen, on the Nette River in the middle Rhineland, was highly valued for the manufacture of grindstones. From early Neolithic times on, the stone was quarried, shaped, and traded. A substantial community exploited this resource during the Roman period, and the extraction of basalt and commerce in the grindstones were carried on continuously from Roman into early medieval times. The roughly shaped stones were transported from Mayen to Andernach, on the Rhine, from which port they were shipped upstream and downstream to communities throughout western and central Europe. The porous quality of Mayen basalt made the stone so highly valued that it was shipped as far as Britain and Denmark.

Most pottery was produced by the communities that used it (chapter 9). Finer wares, favored for serving food by those who could afford them, rather than just for cooking or storage, were manufactured in regional potteries; such wares are often found distributed within twenty or thirty miles of their production places. But some highly specialized pottery-producing communities developed in places where especially fine potting clays were available. At Mayen, in the middle Rhineland, along with the basalt-quarrying industry and trade, a specialized potters' community developed. At the thriving early medieval pottery production site there, twenty kilns have been identified and studied. Mayen pottery was shipped southward up the Rhine to southwestern Germany and Switzerland, and down the river to the lower Rhineland. Substantial quantities were even shipped to lands on the coasts of the North Sea, such as northwestern Germany, and across the English Channel to southeastern England.

At the far extreme from the community-made and locally consumed pottery are the imported luxury wares from beyond Europe. These include wheel-made ornate tablewares from eastern Mediterranean regions, especially Egypt and Turkey, and northern Africa, as well as containers—amphoras—that served for the transport of wine, olive oil, and other luxury comestibles. These imports occur almost exclusively in contexts associated with elites; they clearly mark a completely different system of goods circulation from that of local intervillage exchange of ceramics.

Amber, a fossilized resin from ancient trees, was a favored material for making beads and other ornaments. Women frequently wore necklaces of amber beads or pendants carved from amber. In men's graves, especially from the fifth and sixth centuries, amber beads were sometimes found as pendants on swords and scabbards. In modern times, amber has been regarded as a magical substance and has been worn to protect the wearer from harm. It probably played a similar role in these earlier periods as well.

The principal source of amber in Europe is the coastlands of the Baltic Sea and the North Sea coast of Denmark. The resin derives from ancient forests, now submerged beneath the Baltic. After storms, quantities of amber wash onto the beaches of Denmark, northern Germany, Poland, and the regions along the eastern edges of the Baltic Sea, where it is collected for carving into various desired forms.

The presence of great quantities of exotic luxury goods from distant lands in graves and on settlements of the fifth, sixth, and seventh centuries disproves the notion that trade declined with the end of Roman political domination. I have mentioned the different fine ceramic tablewares from northern Africa and the eastern Mediterranean that are found in many settlements in Europe. Bronze bowls from the eastern Mediterranean regions are well represented in wealthy burials in the upper Danube lands, the middle and lower Rhineland, and Britain. Silk textiles from the Byzantine sphere of the eastern Mediterranean are represented in a number of burials, such as the woman's grave beneath the Cologne Cathedral (chapter 11) and at Niederstotzingen in Württemberg. Belt buckles carved from rock crystal are not unusual in men's burials of the late fifth and early sixth centuries in much of temperate Europe; the great majority of them were manufactured in workshops in the Byzantine eastern Mediterranean region. Unique manufactured objects demonstrate connections over great distances. The bronze Buddha figurine found at the manufacturing and commercial center at Helgö, in central Sweden, was made during the sixth century in the Swat Valley, in northwestern India, some six thousand miles from the spot where archaeologists found it in 1956.

At least some of the garnet that is so abundantly repre-

Figure 10.2. Bronze figure of Buddha, crafted in northern India and found at Helgö, Sweden (height 3¼ inches).

sented on fibulae, sword hilts and scabbards, and other precious ornaments is believed to have been quarried in India and Sri Lanka, though other possible sources are in Bohemia and Scandinavia. Unusually shaped seashells from the Indian Ocean or the Red Sea were perforated and worn by women on bronze rings or chains, probably as amulets, and buried with them in their graves. Ivory was a much-favored material for crafted precious objects for display by elites. Ivory came from the tusks of the African and Indian elephant, as well as those of the walrus and the hippopotamus.

In Gaul and other regions that had been Roman provinces, the practice of minting coins and using them for exchange continued without interruption. Coins circulated even in areas in which none were minted, such as in southwestern Germany. Hundreds of mints are known from Gaul during the fifth through eighth centuries, indicating a much more diffuse system of issuing money than had existed under the centralized control of the Roman emperors. Coins were minted at many of the ports on the coasts of the North and Baltic seas, and they turn up in large quantities on excavated sites. Coins are especially useful indicators of the directions of trade systems, because, unlike many goods, their stamps inform us of where each one was struck.

QUANTITIES OF GOODS

An educated guess estimates that all of the material that we have from the early Middle Ages—in museums, churches, private collections, archaeological research facilities—represents roughly 1 percent of what existed at the time. If this is correct, then the 100 bronze "Coptic" bowls that are known from the sixth century in central regions of Europe would represent some 10,000 bowls that originally arrived from the eastern Mediterranean workshops. Similar ratios can be applied to other categories of objects. Although such an estimate is imperfect, it provides a useful way to think about the scale on which trade moved.

TREASURE

Gold was transported widely throughout Europe. For as long as Rome maintained troops along its frontiers—into the early part of the fifth century—soldiers who served in the auxiliary forces brought their payment in the form of gold coins home with them to different parts of the continent. Roman emperors, both western and eastern, made payments in gold to rulers across the frontier for their services in helping to protect their provinces from invasion. In the case of the eastern Roman emperors based in Constantinople, this practice continued well into the eighth century. Trade played a part in the circulation of gold as well. Plunder was always a mechanism through which gold was moved from one place to another. This precious metal was prized throughout northern Europe for the manufacture of personal ornaments, decorations on weapons, and special items of larger social significance, such as the Gallehus horns—two large and richly ornamented objects from central Denmark that were made around A.D. 400.

A special category of gold objects, often combined with silver objects and precious stones, was "treasure," many examples of which have been found buried in the ground all over Europe. As early as the thirteenth century, the Danish king passed a law stating that any gold found in the ground belonged to the crown—a sure indication that people were finding things.

Many of these treasure deposits had been hidden for safekeeping and for some reason never recovered. The quantities of gold in them—often several pounds—indicates how much of this precious metal was in circulation. Two examples illustrate the character of some of these deposits.

A hoard of gold objects found at Szilágysomlyó, (then in Hungary, now Simleul Silvaniei, in Romania), is one of twenty-eight known gold hoards from the Carpathian basin that were buried during the fifth and sixth centuries. This one included fourteen gold medallions from Rome minted between the end of the third and the end of the fourth century; a gold chain with fifty-two pendants; rings; decorative attachments for belts; and other ornaments. Similar hoards of gold, mostly in the form of Roman coins and medallions, or of local jewelry, are common throughout the continental frontier zones and beyond during the fourth, fifth, and sixth centuries. Many of the hoards probably represent wealth transferred from the late Roman emperors to the barbarian kings across the borders of the Empire.

As the new kingdoms grew in size, power, and wealth between the fourth and sixth centuries, precious metals played an increasing role in the accumulation, transfer, dispersal, and exercise of power. Individuals—we might call them warrior chiefs or kings—who wanted to amass power over their fellows accumulated what precious metal they could. They were able to distribute such wealth to their loyal followers, thereby building up a base of faithful henchmen. After coinage had ceased to be minted by the western Roman emperors, gold metal still retained its economic, political, and social value. The special power of gold is apparent in the surviving tales of the time, such as the epic poem *Beowulf*. In such stories, as well as in the historical accounts of Gregory of Tours and other writers, the great political, social, and even mystical power of gold is apparent.

A different kind of treasure deposit was found in 1837 in the village of Pietroasa, in Romania. It included five gold vessels—a large plate, a jug, a bowl, and two handled beakers—all highly ornate. The beakers include garnets set into cells in the sides of the vessels and the bodies of the leopards that form the handles. Three gold neck rings and four gold fibulae inset with garnets complete the assemblage. The most striking object of the set is a large fibula in the shape of an eagle, bearing complex ornaments of garnet and cabochons. At the bottom are four pendant chains of gold with oval rock crystals at their ends. The Pietroasa hoard shows that treasure was not just gold metal but could include complex and finely crafted ornaments as well. Such hoards often passed from one powerful individual or group to another.

When the armies of powerful kingdoms and empires clashed, their aims were not just to conquer territory but also to acquire wealth. The victors could demand of their defeated enemies the forfeiture of treasure, which was usually in the form of gold, the periodic payment of tribute, or both. Although the surviving written sources from the period say little about everyday manufacturing and trade, they sometimes mention large payments made by kings to rulers whose forces defeated them, or treasures that changed hands as the result of military victory. When Charlemagne won a great victory over a Lombard king in 774, he seized the royal treasure and brought it back to his own kingdom. An account of a treasure that was shipped from the Hungarian Plain, on the middle Danube, back to the Frankish lands in 795—resulting from military victories at that time—mentions fifteen ox-drawn carts filled with silks, silver, and gold.

Such movements of precious metals and other luxury goods represented huge transfers of wealth from one political entity to another. They provided items that the victorious king could give as gifts to his loyal followers. They also constituted the raw material from which much of the personal jewelry, ornamented weapons, and fine tableware were made. They reveal the connections between such transfers of precious metals across Europe and the craft products that archaeologists recover from the richly outfitted burials of the elites, such as those of Childeric (chapter 4), the Anglo-Saxon king at Sutton Hoo (chapter 3), and the woman buried under the Cologne Cathedral (chapter 11).

PROTECTED COMMERCE

Garnet, which was much used to decorate the finest jewelry and weapons of the fifth, sixth, and seventh centuries, is not common on the Earth's surface. A number of known deposits were exploited in this period from Scandinavia to Sri Lanka. In addition to being semiprecious because of its relative rarity, garnet is a hard stone and required highly specialized crafts workers to cut it for inlay. Because gold and garnet ornament occurs only in elite contexts, the specialists in this craft were no doubt few in number relative to those who made bronze fibulae and other more common objects, and they probably worked at only a limited number of crafts centers. Much of the garnet seen in jewelry from all across Europe was probably cut in special workshops at Constantinople, or in some cases in smaller workshops in central and western Europe. From those specialized workshops, the cut stone was carried to less specialized workshops where jewelers set the cut stones into gold fittings.

From this reconstruction of the production and circulation of garnet, it has been argued that this network must have been well organized and supervised, and Europe must have been stable politically for this precious substance to be transported successfully throughout the continent and be locally processed and mounted in many different places. From the example of Eligius as royal jeweler (chapter 9), we can understand how high-level authorities—kings—must have been involved in seeing to it that the circulation systems were not disrupted, as Charlemagne makes clear in his letter to Offa, quoted at the beginning of this chapter. This important point provides another piece of evidence to counter the unfounded notion that the Dark Ages was largely a time of chaos and war.

11
Spread of the New Religion

❖

THIS IS A CUSTOM AMONG THE . . . GAULS WHO are Christians: they send suitable Christian men to the Franks and the other nations with so many thousand *solidi* to ransom baptized people who have been captured. You, on the contrary, murder them [or] sell them to an outlandish race which does not know God.

This quotation from St. Patrick's *Letter to Coroticus* shows the vital role that religion played in people's identity, and even in their physical well-being, during the fifth century, when Patrick was active in Ireland and communities on the continent were struggling to come to terms with the spread of Christianity. Patrick was born and died during the fifth century, but we do not know the exact dates of his birth or death; nor do we know exactly when he spent his roughly thirty years proselytizing for the new religion in Ireland. The passage above from his letter to Coroticus, who was probably a regional king in Scotland, reflects the strife between groups who had accepted the new religion and those that had not. It gives an impression of the kinds of struggles that Patrick faced as he worked to spread Christianity in Ireland sometime around the middle of the fifth century.

Although Patrick is the most famous of the early missionaries to Ireland, he was not the first. According to the written sources, Pope Celestine had sent a man named Palladius to Ireland in 431 as the first bishop there. Patrick's place in the history of the conversion is based on two documents that he wrote—the letter quoted above and his *Confession*—and on a cult that developed around him in the seventh century.

On the other side of Europe, Ulfilas played a somewhat similar role among the Goths. He lived during the fourth century in Asia Minor and southeastern Europe. Although many details about his life are unclear, we know that he translated the Bible from Greek into Gothic, and he is credited with converting many Ostrogoths and Visigoths to Christianity. He ran into problems with the Gothic authorities and lived out his later years with his followers in the late Roman province of Moesia, south of the middle Danube River.

CONVERSION

People do not change their beliefs readily or easily. Even when a ruler proclaims the change of a society's religion, as happened when Constantine made Christianity the official religion of the Roman Empire in 312, or when Queen Elizabeth outlawed the Catholic Church in England in the sixteenth century, most people go on thinking and believing the way they had been. In mid-first-millennium Europe, even after a society had become officially Christian, many people continued to practice traditional ways of conducting rituals. Burial practices of early Christian communities maintained traditions of Roman funerary ritual. Holy relics were used in church settings in ways similar to how foundation sacrifices were employed in Roman times. (In Roman and earlier times, objects including skulls of animals or, occasionally, humans, were sometimes buried beneath the floor of a new building, often near the entrance, as part of a ceremony asking supernatural powers for protection for the structure and its occupants.) Beliefs surrounding early saints in the Christian Church were much like ideas about local spirits inhabiting the countryside in earlier times.

Examining the process of conversion to Christianity is complex and difficult, because no single source of information provides us with a consistent picture of the changing situation. Because nearly all of the written sources about the introduction and spread of Christianity come from officials of the Church (and therefore are unlikely to be strictly objective), we need to look closely at the direct material evidence to learn what people were actually doing in their religious practices. A few examples illustrate the character and complexity of this evidence.

On April 10, 1959, as workmen were digging twenty feet below the choir of the Cologne Cathedral, they came upon an unusually well-preserved and richly outfitted grave of a young woman estimated to have been about twenty-eight years of age at the time of her death around the year 530. The grave had been set within a small chapel of rectangular shape, with an apse extending eastward. The structure was a precursor to today's Cologne Cathedral on the same spot. The western edge of the grave was formed by part of the Roman wall that had been built around the Roman city of Cologne. The stone-lined burial chamber contained the remains of a wooden coffin, at the foot of which stood a number of objects that had been placed in the grave. The whole assemblage had been covered over with a blanket or woolen cloak.

The grave is of particular interest for two reasons besides its extraordinary wealth and its lack of disturbance. Its location, clearly within a small Christian structure, makes it an example of *ad sanctos* burial—interment close to a sacred building or person. But unlike the well-documented Christian graves of slightly later times, this grave included a great wealth of objects buried with the woman—objects that characterized wealthy women of pre-Christian traditions.

The grave included twelve gold coins, eight of them outfitted with eyelets for suspension, apparently on a necklace. On her forehead the woman wore an ornamental band that included gold threads, gold beads, gold-and-garnet ornaments, and silver wire. She wore a pair of gold-and-garnet earrings. On her left wrist was a solid gold bracelet. A gold ring was on one finger on each hand. She wore two pairs of fibulae. One pair is bow fibulae of gold and silver ornamented with an intricate pattern of garnets set into cells formed of gold. The other pair is rosette fibulae of gold and garnet with a cross pattern formed by gold filigree in the center of each. Other ornaments include five pendants of gold with filigree decoration, three gold-and-garnet pendants in the shape of fleur-de-lis, three cloisonné beads, seven gold beads, and nineteen glass beads.

At the foot of the grave, outside the coffin, was a feasting set comprising six glass vessels, including three high-necked bottles, two bowls, and a small beaker. A bronze basin, a drinking horn, and a wooden bucket completed the set. A fragmentary wooden box contained remains of slippers, a ceramic spindle whorl, hazelnut and walnut shells, and a date seed.

This grave includes all of the principal categories of objects that traditionally accompanied wealthy women in their burials during late prehistoric times. The only signs of religious change are the grave's location within an early church structure, and the crosses formed by the ornament on the two rosette fibulae and on the top of the knife handle. Although the decoration on the rosette fibulae refers to the new religious symbolism that was being introduced around this time, the patterned ornament on the two bow fibulae suggests something different. Special attention has been called to a series of marvelously complex patterns of animal ornament on these fibulae; they were constructed in such a way as to be hidden from all but initiates. It is a bit like the complex drawings in which children are instructed to find ten animals hidden in the foliage, but here it is basic abstract elements of the animals that we need to find. In the center of the head end of the fibulae are two overlapping heads of birds of prey in side view, sharing an eye. The eye also forms the center of a flying insect, its antennae and wings represented by the upper and lower borders of the center section of the fibula head.

This juxtaposition of Christian imagery on one pair of fibulae and of non-Christian, traditional animal imagery on the other pair raises interesting questions about change and continuity in religious ideas in the context of this extraordinary early sixth-century burial. The syncretism of the two different belief systems apparent on the fibulae in this grave is a good example of the complexity of the development of the new religion in the context of existing ideas, beliefs, and symbols.

STYLE, ANIMALS, AND CHRISTIANITY

What was the relation between the new Christian symbolism and the traditional motifs and designs in ornament, and what can this relationship tell us about the acceptance of the new religion? Animal representations on personal ornaments can be traced far into prehistoric times. Especially on fibulae, but on other jewelry such as neck rings, bracelets, finger rings, and pendants as well, the heads of birds, cattle, pigs, horses, and mythical creatures that combine features of different animals are especially common. In regions of Europe conquered by the Roman armies, the popularity of animal ornament declined somewhat, but in unconquered areas it remained important. Then in the latter part of the Roman period, new animal ornament became immensely popular, borrowing styles from Roman themes and integrating them with local fashions.

The newly flourishing designs of the fifth and sixth centuries can be understood in relation to the forming of new political identities among the peoples of central and northern Europe. According to this argument, the ornament references foundational myths about the formation of new nations—stories that explain how the nation came into being and why the rulers are who they are—at the time that Roman control was waning and new kingdoms were coming into being beyond and within the old imperial borders.

A religious interpretation of the animal art of this period can also be put forward. The animal style that emerged in northern Europe has been understood as reflecting "different modes of representation" from those of early Christianity. The proliferation of the animal style at this time may have been in deliberate reaction to the representations that were being created in the late Roman world in the imperial provinces. Whereas

Roman representation tended to be narrative—to tell stories—the animal style of ornament was instead symbolic and, it is important to add, difficult for outsiders to read. This is not to say that these stylized animals may not also have been parts of stories, only that we cannot interpret those stories as well as we can the more familiar Roman imagery and narrative. Many of the animal representations show ambiguous creatures; we are not sure what exactly they are intended to represent, if they were intended to represent any particular kind of creatures at all. This line of argument would be consistent with the idea that many communities in Europe, especially those north of the old Roman frontier line at the Rhine and Danube, did not begin to seriously adopt the new religion until much later than some of the areas within the Roman lands, and many actively resisted the symbols of the new religion as well as the substance and practices. In resisting, they reached back into earlier times, even to the prehistoric Iron Age, to adapt and recreate iconography that would serve their purposes.

BORROWING FROM THE PAST

We can learn much about the spread of Christianity and how it supplanted earlier religious beliefs and practices through examination of early Christian churches. In the stone wall of the church of Notre-Dame du Puy, in the French department of Haute-Loire, archaeologists found numerous Roman period sculptures in classic Gallo-Roman style. They included scenes in relief, inscriptions, and architectural elements. Roman sculptures associated with medieval church foundations are not unusual, but this case is special for two reasons. Le Puy has no evidence of having been a Roman settlement. Everything indicates that the town was founded in early medieval times. The sculptures thus cannot have been of local origin but must have been brought from somewhere else, perhaps from Saint-Paulien, eight miles away. In addition, no other Roman sculptures have been found at Le Puy except those in the cathedral and associated buildings. In other words, the carved stones in the walls of Notre-Dame du Puy were apparently not brought simply as convenient building material that was similarly used elsewhere in the town.

While excavating beneath the great medieval Christian cathedral at Bonn, in the Rhineland in Germany, in 1928–1930, archaeologists came upon a cemetery that had been used during the Roman period and early medieval times. Among the architectural remains associated with the graves were some seventy stone sculptures of the Roman period. These included representations of the standard Roman gods and goddesses but also large numbers of sculptures of the indigenous deities, especially mother goddesses, that had been revered in this region before and during the Roman period.

At the former Roman military and civil site of Uley, in Gloucestershire in western England, a Roman-style temple was dismantled sometime around the middle of the fifth century. Fragments of a major statue from the temple were reused in the construction of a timber-frame building on the site; others became part of the foundation of a later church, but the head was kept separate. This sculpted head was buried by itself in a pit sometime after the rest of the statue fragments had been reused to construct the church foundation.

These three examples show special attention paid to dismantled Roman religious monuments. The reuse of elements of those monuments indicates something much more complex than a break between pre-Christian Roman religious traditions and the adoption and eager practice of the new religion of Christianity.

In trying to understand past ritual and religion, it is important to distinguish between what the written evidence indicates and what the material evidence reveals. Textual evidence can tell us much about "official" religions and how they should be practiced, about the attributes of different deities, and so forth, but they are not good sources for how people actually behaved. As we shall see throughout this chapter, people in early Europe carried out a wide range of different kinds of ritual practices, only a few of which are understandable with reference to the official religions other than those of the pre-Christian Roman Empire or Christianity. For the question of transition from religions of the Roman period to Christianity of the early medieval period, the most important point is the persistence throughout of ritual practices that were not necessarily connected to the official Roman pantheon or to Christianity but survived and developed in the private traditions of the early Europeans.

REPRESENTING NEW THEMES

Two symbols of Christianity are distinctive in the late Roman and early medieval contexts: the cross and the chi-rho, the two letters that begin the name Christ in Greek. Both occur in a variety of media from the fourth century on. The cross sometimes appears in the form of small cross-shaped objects, such as the gold foil crosses just a couple of inches across that are often found on the lower part of the face in graves from the late sixth and seventh centuries. Crosses often ornament other objects, such as ceramic lamps, boxes made of bone, and even sword scabbards. The chi-rho symbol often decorates objects such as medallions. Throughout the late Roman and early medieval periods, the signs of the new religion consistently occur together with other, non-Christian material, not in contexts that we would immediately recognize as "fully Christian."

In what has been described as one of the earliest representations of Christ as a person, the figure of a young man occurs in a mosaic at Hinton St. Mary, in Dorset, England. This mosaic, discovered in a field in 1963, covered the floor of a room measuring about twenty-eight by twenty feet in a villa. The mosaic shows a young man wearing a toga-like garment, and behind his head is the chi-rho sign. Surrounding this head, which is believed to represent Christ, are hunting scenes, busts of four other men, and the classical representation of Bellerophon fighting the goat-headed monster known as the Chimera. Of special interest here is the integration of an early representation of Christ into a Roman medium—the mosaic floor of a country villa—with traditional scenes from typical Roman mosaic floors. Unusual is the representation of Christ on a floor, where people were likely to walk.

In many contexts, objects bearing important Christian symbols were integrated with the long-standing practice of making ritual deposits of valuable metalwork in the ground and in bodies of water. At Water Newton, near Peterborough, in Cambridgeshire, a hoard of gold and silver objects was found in 1975. These included nine silver vessels, sixteen silver plaques, and a gold disk. Metal vessels and gold and silver ornaments had been deposited in great numbers all over Europe from the Bronze Age through the Iron Age and the Roman period. The purpose of these deposits is generally thought to be votive; they were intended as offerings to gods or spirits as parts of ritual ceremonies. Sheet silver plaques are a common form of votive offering in Roman provincial contexts, where they frequently bear representations of Roman gods and goddesses. The silver plaques in the Water Newton find, several of which are gilded, are unusual in that they bear unmistakably Christian signs: chi-rho symbols and, on one, an inscription that attests to the votive function of the object—AMCILLA VOTUM QUO(D) PROMISIT CONPLEVIT ("Amcilla has completed her vow that she promised"). Two of the silver cups and the strainer also bear inscriptions that attest to their function here as objects dedicated to Christ. We see therefore in this find, described as "the earliest surviving liturgical plate from the Early Church from anywhere in the Roman Empire," the use of a standard Roman period medium (the silver plaques) for purposes of representing the new religion, and, in the deposition of this assemblage of precious metal objects in the ground, the continuation of an ancient practice of dedicating valued goods to deities.

A hoard of precious metal objects discovered in 1992 at Hoxne, in East Anglia in southern England, contained 14,865 gold and silver coins and a couple of hundred other items made of these metals. Of special significance here are objects that bear inscriptions. Two of the silver spoons in the hoard bear the chi-rho symbol. A necklace, two spoons, and two ladles have on them a monogram cross. Another spoon bears the words VIVAS IN DEO ("May you live in God"). All of these inscribed signs and words suggest that the person or group that owned this series of objects deposited at Hoxne had close connections with Christianity in the early fifth century, when the hoard was buried.

Finally, a richly outfitted woman's burial at Wittislingen, in southwest Germany, contained a cross of sheet gold and a highly ornate gilded silver fibula with garnet inlay and a

Latin inscription on the back that is interpreted as a sign of Christianity. This grave is unusual in that the woman's name is given in the inscription. It translates as "May Uffila, taken by death, live happily in God, for throughout my life I have been pious. Rest in God." The fibula bearing this inscription is decorated with a pair of heads of birds of prey on the front and a snake on the back. A round silver amulet box from the grave bears interlaced animal ornament. Thus, like the Cologne woman's burial, this one, dated around A.D. 600, shows the mixing of new Christian themes with a traditional symbolic repertoire. In the wealth of gold and silver in the grave, the entire complex is very different from what later becomes the standard form of Christian burial.

DIVERSE PRACTICES

Water has long played a major role in religious ritual practice, and many places in Europe show continuous use of watery sites from pre-Christian into Christian times. An example is the confluence of the Naab River into the Danube River just upstream from the city of Regensburg, in Bavaria, Germany. Numerous objects have been dredged up from the bottom of the Naab and from the Danube here, including complete ceramic vessels, bronze ornaments, and iron weapons, all spanning the millennia from the Neolithic period to the High Middle Ages. Not coincidently, on the point of land next to the confluence stands an ornate pilgrimage church, known as Mariaort ("place of the Virgin Mary"). Thus the function of this place—this confluence of rivers—as a site for ritual practice has been preserved into modern times from the late Stone Age. This case is not exceptional.

Figure 11.1. The pilgrimage church of Mariaort, situated at the confluence of the Naab River into the Danube just west of Regensburg, southern Germany. This river confluence has been an important site of ritual activity for at least three thousand years. A variety of bronze and iron objects, including especially swords, has been dredged from the river confluence here. The construction of a Christian church here shows that the site preserved its ritual significance, even as the dominant religion changed.

During the Viking period (A.D. 800–1100) in England, large numbers of swords were thrown into rivers. A forty-year-old study identified thirty-four instances of swords being found in rivers, twenty-two of them from the Thames. By this time,

England was officially a Christian land. Throwing weapons into water had no sanctioned role in Christian religious practice. But the direct evidence of all of these finds shows that people were carrying on this old practice well into the Middle Ages.

At Oberdorla, in Thuringia in eastern Germany, long-term archaeological research has uncovered a place where ritual structures were erected and ritual activities, involving sacrificing animals and humans and depositing offerings, were practiced for more than a thousand years, from the early Iron Age into the early Middle Ages. The site consists of a pond surrounded by a bog, and over the millennia platforms were built up of earth, fires were burned on the platforms, and animals were sacrificed and their skeletal remains deposited in pits. A variety of different crafted objects, including carved human figures of wood, were arranged on the site. In the Middle Ages, the importance of place in the memory of local people is reflected in special status given to the church established here. There have even been suggestions that special practices carried out by the Christian community at Oberdorla can be traced directly to the rituals conducted at the pre-Christian sacred site. In a spring ceremony performed in the local town, a boy is led in a procession inside a great basket woven of reeds, similar to objects preserved in the bog deposit at Oberdorla. The idea of the worship of a nature goddess, akin to the Roman Diana, goddess of the forest, is also identifiable well into Christian times in the area. One account of the martyrdom of St. Kilian, an Irish monk who, with two companions, was murdered in the area about the year 689, suggests that the perpetrators were members of a cult that worshipped this goddess and took offense at the proselytizing monk.

The site of Tara in Ireland, just west of Dublin, is rich with pre-Christian and Christian associations. The site survives today as a ridgetop concentration of some forty sites recognizable on the surface. These include mounds, banked enclosures, and various linear earthworks. Ritual activity on the site dates back to the Neolithic period (4000 B.C.), and practices were still being carried out during the early Christian Middle Ages. In Irish tradition, Tara was the place where the most powerful kings of Ireland were inaugurated. Much of the ritual connected with these royal rites seems to have involved fertility symbols and associations. Because of the powerful non-Christian ritual links of the site, the early Christian Church made efforts to suppress the activity and the traditions connected with it. Surviving documents suggest that Tara was probably still the inauguration site of kings during the eighth century, and perhaps into the ninth, as the Ui Neill dynasty assumed power over all of Ireland.

CONTINUITY

When Christianity was introduced at different times in different places, it did not erase earlier traditions of ritual or belief. As the examples cited above indicate, elements of the new religion appeared integrated with elements of other traditions. Although "Roman" and "Christian" religions came into temperate Europe from outside, both were overlays that did not replace existing beliefs and practices but rather added to and complemented them.

Today we see the persistence of many of these practices that go back to well before the time of the Romans. Wearing or carrying charms, saying prayers before meals, decorating Christmas trees, coloring eggs at Easter, and tossing coins into fountains are parts of practices that were carried out by the prehistoric peoples of Europe. What people think today when they toss their pennies, dimes, and quarters into the water may not be very different from what eighth-century Britons thought as they threw their swords into the Thames at London.

The spread of Christianity from the fifth century on had a major impact not just on Europeans' beliefs and ritual practices but also on artistic activity, scholarship, and writing, as we shall see in the next chapter.

12
Arts, Scholarship, and Education

❖

He was zealous in his cultivation of the liberal arts . . . He learned grammar from the Deacon Peter of Pisa . . . Alcuin, a man of Saxon origin who came from Britain and was the greatest scholar of his time, taught him the other subjects. . . . [T]he king spent a great deal of time and effort studying rhetoric, logic, and especially astronomy.

This passage from Einhard's *Life of Charlemagne* reveals the intellectual richness of Charlemagne's empire at the end of the eighth century and of the distances from which Charlemagne brought great scholars and teachers to create the lively artistic and intellectual environment known as the Carolingian Renaissance. How did this development come about? Was it the only such flowering of art, architecture, education, scholarship, and writing since the time of the Roman Empire, or did

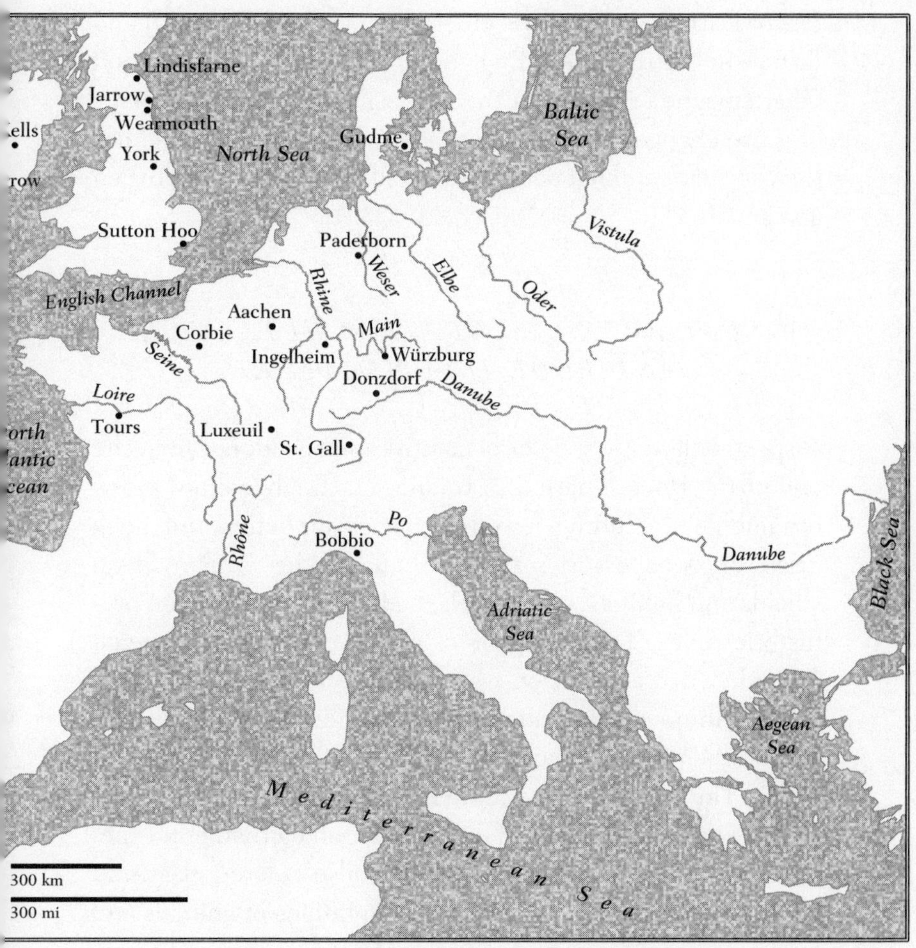

Figure 12.1. Places mentioned in chapter 12.

a similar flourishing of arts and learning emerge at different times and different places?

As this chapter shows, from the fifth century on major new developments in the arts, architecture, scholarship, writing, and education took place in Europe. A few major centers of learning and culture emerged, such as Wearmouth and Jarrow, in Northumbria, England, in the seventh century and Charlemagne's Aachen in the late eighth century. But many of these changes took place at different locations throughout the continent and happened during all four centuries between 400 and 800.

VISUAL ARTS: DECORATIVE METALWORK AND BOOK ILLUMINATION

A spectacular new style of decorative metalwork began at the end of the Roman period. A tradition of finely crafted metal ornaments, including jewelry such as brooches and neck rings, dress accessories such as belt buckles, ornament on shields and helmets, and vessels, had persisted since late prehistoric times. The new style of metalworking that emerged from the fifth century on was based in large part on motifs and techniques that had been used since the Iron Age but also on themes and practices of metal craft in the late Roman world. The special elements that characterize this new style include chip-carving of surfaces; polychrome ornament, especially in the form of cut garnets, but also colored glass and enamel; integration of stylized representations of animals and humans in the decorative patterns; intertwined animal forms that could be extremely complex; and an emphasis on high relief that often created a sense of three-dimensionality (see chapters 3 and 9).

Three examples from many thousands of possible objects illustrate the character of this new unique artistic craft.

Two identical fibulae that exemplify the new style were found in a woman's richly appointed grave at Donzdorf, in

Figure 12.2. Fibula from Donzdorf, in southwestern Germany (about 5½ inches).

southwestern Germany. The fibulae are about five and a half inches long and made of silver, gold, and garnet. The base metal for each one is silver; most, but not all, of the surface is covered with gold. The raised portions of the ornament emerge from the gold background as bright gleaming silver, creating a three-dimensional appearance to the objects. Twelve finely cut, bright red garnets held in small gold settings, in the technique known as cloisonné, add color and further three-dimensionality to the pieces. Each fibula has eighteen recognizable, though highly stylized, faces as part of the decoration; most of them are human-like, but some look like animals, perhaps horses. Thin, raised spiral and figure-eight patterns, some silver and some gold, fill the few available open spaces on the surface of the fibulae. With this rich decoration of animate faces and limbs, polychrome ornament, high relief, intertwined elements, and spirals, the Donzdorf fibulae exemplify the ornamental style known as "animal ornament" and "Germanic art," which made possible later developments such as Irish book illumination (see below) and, in later centuries, Viking art. The Donzdorf fibulae were made around the year 550. Because the style and technique were so widespread, we do not know precisely where they were made, although the workshop was probably somewhere in what is now France or Germany.

The helmet made of iron, bronze, silver, gold, and garnet that was found in Grave 1 at Sutton Hoo, in East Anglia, England, was manufactured around the year 600. Especially noteworthy for our purposes here are the animal representations and the scenes of warriors decorating the helmet. Broad, bronze eyebrows inlaid with silver wire extend across the face above the eye holes; they end in gilded boar's heads, readily identifiable by the shape of the snout and the upward-pointing tusks. The bronze crest that runs over the top of the helmet terminates at the front and back in gilded serpents' heads with eyes of bright red garnet. A third such head extends upward from the bridge of the nosepiece to meet the head at the front end of the crest. Attached to the outer surface over most of the helmet are small plates of bronze foil coated with tin. Some of these plates bear relief figures of what are described by investigators as dancing warriors. Two men are wearing helmets that are crested by two opposing heads of birds of prey. Each man holds two downward-pointing spears in one hand and a raised sword in the other. Other plates show a warrior on horseback carrying a lance and shield and riding over a fallen man who is holding a sword. The majority of plates bear intricately intertwined animal ornament rather than scenes that include humans.

The third example is a vessel crafted for service in the Christian Church. The Ardagh Chalice, made sometime around the year 725, was found as part of a treasure deposit at Ardagh, in County Limerick, Ireland. The body of the vessel is made of silver, with parts of gold and parts of bronze; it is decorated with glass and rock crystal, stands six inches high, and has two silver handles. Just below the rim is a relief band with lavish intertwined animal ornament made of thin strands of gold; the band is interrupted by circular knobs of patterned silver together with inset blue and red glass. On two sides of the chalice are complex roundels containing delicate gold filigree and five ornamental knobs—a large central knob with blue and red glass arranged in settings outlined in silver, and four glass-filled knobs around the perimeter. The stem that connects the bowl with its base is covered with intricately ornamented gold. On the shoulder of the bowl, just below the decorative band, the names of the apostles are engraved; between the letters are tiny dots produced with a fine punch and a hammer, creating a sense of three-dimensionality for the lettering.

All three of these masterpieces of metal crafting, each produced in a different part of Europe, show important artistic connections with the book illumination that developed at the same time. The common elements in metalwork and the art of the new books underscore the universality of the new motifs and decorative patterns and unite these different artistic expressions through common meanings. The ornament on the Ardagh Chalice shows particularly strong links with the decoration of the Book of Durrow, the Lindisfarne Gospels, and the Book of Kells, discussed below.

Book illumination—adding pictures to texts—did not begin in Europe until the start of the fifth century. The manuscript scrolls that were the typical Roman medium of recording written information were not illustrated. The tradition of book illustration in this period began in Ireland, at the far northwestern corner of Europe, shortly after the conversion of the island to Christianity. It is significant that much of the metalwork in the new style, such as the Donzdorf fibulae and the Sutton Hoo helmet discussed above, have no apparent links with the new religion. But book illustration was a highly Christian phenomenon. The pictures were created specifically to illustrate religious texts, and the subjects of the illustrations—representations of Christ and the Apostles, especially—were closely linked to those texts. On the other hand, even the book illustrations contain abundant decorative elements—often filling entire pages—that are in no recognizable way specifically Christian and instead refer back to pre-Christian themes and designs.

Religious leaders developed their own distinctive script, the earliest traces of which date to the latter part of the sixth century. One of the earliest written documents to display the new style of manuscript illumination is the Cathach, a Psalter consisting of fifty-eight sheets of vellum—laboriously prepared skins of calves, sheep, or goats. Of particular importance is the greatly enlarged letter that begins each Psalm, characteristically ornamented in the La Tène style of Celtic artistic tradition that was richly exhibited on metalwork from 500 B.C. on. The fully developed style of manuscript illumination is displayed in the Book of Durrow, painted around the middle of the seventh century in central Ireland. As on metalwork, especially of the fifth and sixth centuries, interwoven animal ornament and patterns of spirals and trumpet shapes characterize the illustrated pages in this book.

The Irish monasteries at which scribes and artists produced these extraordinary objects sent missions to other parts of Europe, most notably across the Irish Sea to Northumbria, in northern England, and to the Frankish regions on the continent. The Irish-founded monastery on the island of Lindisfarne, on the east coast of Northumbria, was to become one of the most important centers of artistic production, scholarship, and teaching. The Lindisfarne Gospels, produced around the year 720, is one of the most complete and best preserved of the illuminated books created by specialists trained in the Irish tradition. This highly illustrated book is thought to have been made by a single individual who did the writing and painting over the course of some five years. The skins of about 130 calves were used to make the pages of the book.

The most spectacular of all the surviving illuminated book manuscripts is the Book of Kells, made around the middle of the eighth century in Ireland. It presents the four gospels. The illustrations include representations of Jesus and Mary, portraits of Christ as an adult, initial letters elaborately decorated with intertwined animals in the Celtic style, and fantastically complex "carpet pages" of exceedingly detailed intertwined ornament. Unlike the Lindisfarne Gospels, the Book of Kells is thought to have involved the hands of several scribes and artists. The complexity and richness of the illustrations are more extreme than those of any other book produced in Europe in this period. The ornament borrows from the earlier traditions of decorative metalwork and adds new levels of detail, as well as including for the first time numerous whole human figures in the ornamental patterns.

On the European continent, post-Roman book illumination began later than it did in Ireland. The earliest manuscript that includes such decoration comes from Luxeuil, in east-central France, and dates to the year 669. The distinctive style developed on the continent is characterized by the use of the compass to draw circles and by simple images of fish and birds decorating initial letters. A related tradition of ornamentation emerged at Corbie, in northern France, as well as at other locations within the Frankish empire during the first half of the eighth century.

ARCHITECTURE

As with the new styles of metalwork and book illumination, new architectural features developed between 400 and 800 that borrowed elements from local and Mediterranean traditions. Though the great halls of earlier times in northern Europe, such as that at the political and religious center of Gudme, in Denmark (chapter 7), were constructed of timber, large rectangular stone-built architectural spaces came to characterize new buildings of political and religious importance in the early medieval period. A striking example is the palace constructed by Charlemagne at Aachen as the monumental edifice from which to administer his empire. The basilica of Constantine at Trier is often cited as a model for Charlemagne's palace, but the earlier halls of northern Europe also played major roles as prototypes (chapters 3 and 7). The building materials—stone and cement—were of Roman character, but the form and function of such halls had developed within local societies over the centuries. The form of the large rectangular hall also served as the basis for Charlemagne's other imperial palaces, at Ingelheim and Paderborn. The same architectural configuration formed the centerpiece for the monumental monastery at St. Gall, in Switzerland, the detailed plan of which is regarded as a key piece in the emergence of this new architecture of the early Middle Ages. On a smaller scale, the basic hall shape was adopted for use in churches constructed throughout Christian Europe.

The vast majority of buildings from this period do not survive, most of them having been dismantled long ago to make way for new construction. But archaeological excavations have uncovered the foundations of many of the structures built between 400 and 800. The surviving plan for a monastery at St. Gall is unique in providing a detailed architectural drawing, on five pieces of parchment with total dimensions of forty-five by thirty-one inches. It shows the monumental scale on which builders were thinking for the new religious architecture at the start of the ninth century.

SCHOLARSHIP AND WRITING

Although from the period known as the Dark Ages there are fewer texts dealing with historical subjects than from earlier and later times, the art of writing never completely disappeared. It was kept alive in the scriptoria of monasteries—the rooms in which monks worked copying by hand manuscripts that concerned religious subjects and church activities as well as secular texts from the ancient world. In some cases these included texts that recorded local traditions, such as those that preserved the myths and legends of early Ireland. But most scholarship and writing during this period were based on the needs of the Church and Christianity.

Already in the fifth century, Ireland had become a leading center of Christian scholarship as well as the production of the illuminated manuscripts discussed above. Ireland's early church leaders were in close contact with Christian communities throughout Europe, and they played a major role in sending missions to introduce, or reintroduce, Christianity to other parts of the continent. I have mentioned above the Irish missions to Northumbria in connection with the spread of the Irish tradition of manuscript illumination. Irish monks also established numerous important monasteries on the continent—for example, at Luxeuil, in east-central France; at St. Gall, in Switzerland; at Würzburg, in southern Germany; and at Bobbio, in northern Italy. All of these places developed into major centers of scholarship, writing, and teaching. Columbanus, who was born about 545 in Leinster, in Ireland, was a particularly active missionary responsible for founding three monasteries in France—at Annegrey, in the Vosges region, and at Luxeuil and Fontaine.

The most prominent scholar of this period was Bede, a man of Anglo-Saxon origins who was born in northern England about 672 and died in 735. At the age of seven he entered the monastery that was based at the neighboring sites of Wearmouth and Jarrow, in Northumbria, just at the time that this monastic complex was reaching its apex of cultural achievement. The library at the monastery contained some five hundred books, making it one of the most extensive in Europe at the time. Bede read the classical authors as well as the few earlier English writers such as Gildas, who wrote in the 540s. Bede was widely respected as a thorough researcher who cited extensive references in his works and checked his facts carefully. He is best known today for his five-volume *Ecclesiastical History of the English People,* a work that has formed an essential background for all subsequent histories of England. That great work covers political as well as religious matters, from Julius Caesar's writings about Britain around 50 B.C. to the time that Bede completed the project, in the year 731. Although Bede did not travel abroad, in contrast to the Irish and Anglo-Saxon missionaries who ranged widely over the continent, his written works were well known and highly regarded internationally.

EDUCATION

All of the monasteries, and other centers of scholarship, writing, and artistic production that were associated with them, were institutions where teaching took place. Monasteries taught the young monks who joined them, and often other young men and boys who might possibly have become monks. The emphasis in monastic and church education was, of course, the teachings of the church, but because in the scriptoria the monks were copying other texts besides religious ones, a great deal of secular information was also disseminated at the monastic schools.

By the latter part of the sixth century, more formal educational procedures were appearing in different parts of Europe. The educator about whom we know the most is Alcuin, who was born in 732 and died in 804. He was Northumbrian and was educated at York in the scholarly milieu of Bede and his followers. In 767 Alcuin became director of the substantial monastic library at York and later was placed in charge of the cathedral school in that city. He became famous throughout Christian Europe as a teacher, and in 781 or 782 Charlemagne recruited him to become the director of the palace school at Aachen. From the year 796 on, Alcuin was also abbot of the monastery of St. Martin, in the French city of Tours. His influence on education and scholarship among members of monastic communities and members of the lay public was enormous. He is credited with reorganizing and reinvigorating classical education and church-based learning in Europe, and with restructuring the way that Latin was used in late eighth- and early ninth-century Europe. An extensive collection of his writings survives, including numerous poems, essays, and letters.

The developments between 400 and 800 in the visual arts of ornamental metalwork and book illumination and in architecture, scholarship, and education led gradually, and in different ways in different parts of Europe, to the blossoming of all aspects of "high culture" known as the Carolingian Renaissance. From this time, in the early ninth century, historians trace a direct line to the High Middle Ages, the Renaissance, the Enlightenment, and into modern times. As I have emphasized in this chapter, the early stages of development of these phenomena are often not treated by historians of medieval Europe because, with written sources so sparse, only material evidence can fill in the important gaps.

13
Charlemagne's Elephant and the History of Europe

❖

THE ABBASID CALIPH HARUN AL-RASHID, RULER OF the Muslim world, who was based in Baghdad, dispatched his ambassador, Ibrahim Ibn al-Aghlab, to bring an elephant to Charlemagne at his court in Aachen, in northern Germany. The elephant, named Abu l'Abbas, was a diplomatic gift from the emperor of one part of the world to the emperor of another. This unusual present shows that Charlemagne and his Frankish empire were in close political contact with the greatest power of the Mediterranean world and the Near East. It also shows that the ruler of the Muslim world considered Charlemagne of such stature and authority that he merited an extraordinary royal gift.

Throughout this book, I have tried to show that, far from being a period of cultural bleakness and unmitigated violence, the centuries known popularly as the Dark Ages were a time of dynamic development, cultural creativity, and long-distance networking. Charlemagne's elephant, and all of the other signs of interconnectedness between northern Europe and other parts of the world, attest to the importance of those developments between the disintegration of the Roman Empire and the flowering of Carolingian Europe in the late eighth and ninth centuries.

The Roman Empire "fell" only in the minds of people who had a particular and limited view of what the Roman Empire was and who understood events such as Alaric's capture of Rome in A.D. 410 as marking its end. Similarly, the start of the Migration period, shortly after the appearance in texts of the Huns, in A.D. 375 and the beginning of the Middle Ages, with the formation of the Merovingian dynasty in the middle of the fifth century, are artificial chronological markers that historians created as benchmarks, although they have taken on lives of their own. Too often, modern researchers lose sight of the fact that these fixed points are intended only to provide a framework for understanding peoples of the past, not real breaks in the social or cultural development of early Europeans.

For the auxiliary soldier serving on the Rhine frontier at the end of the Roman period, for farmers in villages in central France, and for the elites at northern centers such as Gudme, in Denmark, and Helgö, in Sweden, there was no abrupt fall of the imperial power. The changes that were taking place from the fifth to the eighth century were gradual; they would not have been perceived as abrupt or transformational to anyone living at the time. It is the way we think about change in the past, and the way we sometimes place too much faith in texts concerning warfare and mass movements of people, that can lead us astray. If we examine instead the material evidence left by people who lived during those centuries, we come to a very different understanding of what those times were like.

Here in this short final chapter, I briefly touch on a question of fundamental importance for understanding the past, and indeed the present, in human societies. The approach to the past for which I have argued here is a "bottom-up" one rather than the traditional "top-down" approach. We can best understand the first millennium in Europe by examining the experiences and practices of the majority of people who lived during those centuries rather than focusing on the Roman emperors, the Germanic chiefs and kings, and other great men of historical tradition. An archaeological approach lends itself to examining majority populations, whereas studies based on texts tend toward understandings centered on the elites' motivations, decisions, and actions.

The big question to which these considerations lead us is, which people drive change? Is change brought about largely through the actions of leaders, or by the majority of people? To read traditional text-based history of the first millennium, we would think that the persons named in the texts were the decisive factors—emperors such as Constantine and Julian, Germanic leaders such as Alaric and Clovis, other barbarian rulers such as Attila. These individuals and their actions were the subjects of the writers' attention; hence, they form the focus of the textual accounts. But battles were won by armies, not by generals. Surplus production by farmers in villages all over Europe enabled the thriving trade in amber and glass beads, grindstones, fine pottery and glassware, and other desirable goods. Growth in manufacturing at centers such as Helgö and Southampton, and at inland settlements such as Mayen, fueled the desire for manufactured goods and trade items throughout Europe. Expansion of specialized industries, such as that in pottery in the middle Rhineland, had no obvious elite component as a driving force. So which group played the greater role in causing the changes during these centuries—the elites or the majority of people?

Unlike most objects that circulated over long-distance commercial routes, Charlemagne's elephant was mentioned in the Frankish chronicles because it was an unusual gift from the principal potentate in the Near East to the ruling emperor of western Europe. But the elephant's arrival in the royal court at Aachen comes as no great surprise to us, given what the archaeological evidence shows about the persistence of long-distance communications and the rise of the new kingdoms of Europe after the disintegration of Rome as a power.

Appendix: Selected Museum Collections

❖

Museums all over Europe hold collections and display objects related to the subject matter of this book. Among the many outstanding exhibitions are those at the following museums. Museum locations, hours, and information about the collections can be found easily on the Internet.

Austria

Naturhistorisches Museum (Natural History Museum), Vienna

Denmark

Moesgård Museum, Højbjerg
Nationalmuseet (National Museum), Copenhagen

France

Musée des Antiquités Nationales (National Museum of Antiquities), Saint-Germain-en-Laye (outside Paris)

Germany

Archäologisches Landesmuseum (State Archaeological Museum), Schleswig

Archäologisches Staatssammlung (State Archaeological Collection), Munich

Rheinisches Landesmuseum (Rhineland Museum), Bonn

Rheinisches Landesmuseum (Rheinland Museum), Trier

Römisch-Germanisches Museum (Roman-Germanic Museum), Cologne

Wikinger Museum Haithabu (Viking Museum Haithabu), Schleswig

Württembergisches Landesmuseum (Württemberg State Museum), Stuttgart

Hungary

Magyar Nemzeti Múzeum (Hungarian National Museum), Budapest

Ireland

National Museum of Ireland, Dublin

Sweden

Historiska Museet (Historical Museum), University of Lund, Lund

Statens Historiska Museum (Museum of National Antiquities), Stockholm

United Kingdom

British Museum, British Library, and Museum of London, all in London

National Museum of Wales, Cardiff

National Museums of Scotland, Edinburgh

Sources and Suggestions for Further Reading

❖

Preface

The quotations are from Edward Gibbon, *The History of the Decline and Fall of the Roman Empire,* ed. by J. B. Bury (London: Postlethwaite, Taylor & Knowles, 1909), vol. 1, chapter 1, p. 1, and chapter 2, pp. 54–55; vol. 5, chapter 30, p. 166. (The original publication dates of Gibbon's six-volume work were 1776–89.)

1 Between Antiquity and the Middle Ages: What Happened?

Characteristic discussions of the idea of the Dark Ages are in W. P. Ker, *The Dark Ages* (New York: New American Library, 1958) and M. Wood, *In Search of the Dark Ages* (London: BBC Books, 1994). Recent scholarly treatments of the period include E. James, *The Franks* (New York: Basil Blackwell, 1988), E. James, *Britain in the First Millennium* (London: Arnold, 2001); P. J. Geary, *Before France and Germany: The Creation and Transformation of the Merovingian World* (New York: Oxford University

Press, 1988), R. McKitterick, ed., *The Early Middle Ages: Europe 400–1000* (Oxford: Oxford University Press, 2001), T. Charles-Edwards, *After Rome* (Oxford: Oxford University Press, 2003), J. M. H. Smith, *Europe After Rome: A New Cultural History 500–1000* (New York: Oxford University Press, 2005), C. Wickham, *Framing the Early Middle Ages: Europe and the Mediterranean 400–800* (New York: Oxford University Press, 2005), and W. Goffart, *Barbarian Tides: The Migration Age and the Later Roman Empire* (Philadelphia: University of Pennsylvania Press, 2006). For discussion of the prominent authors of the period, see Goffart, *The Narrators of Barbarian History (A.D. 550–800): Jordanes, Gregory of Tours, Bede, and Paul the Deacon* (Princeton: Princeton University Press, 1988). Piranesi's etchings are presented in L. Ficacci, *Giovanni Battista Piranesi: The Complete Etchings* (New York: Taschen, 2000). On the Enlightenment, K. Sloan, ed., *Enlightenment: Discovering the World in the Eighteenth Century* (London: British Museum, 2003). The quotation from Ammianus Marcellinus is from the translation by J. C. Rolfe, vol. 3 (Cambridge, Mass.: Harvard University Press, 1972), XXXI 2, 1–11, pp. 381–87. The quotation from St. Jerome is from J. and J. M. Todd, *Voices from the Past* (London: Phoenix House, 1955), p. 523. On Charlemagne and his projects, J. Boussard, *The Civilization of Charlemagne,* trans. by F. Partridge (New York: McGraw-Hill, 1968), and R. Collins, *Charlemagne* (Toronto: University of Toronto, 1998), are useful summaries. Offa's Dyke: D. H. Hill, "Offa's Dyke: Pattern and Purpose," *Antiquaries Journal* 80 (2000), pp. 195–206. Danevirke: H. H. Andersen et al., *Danevirke*, 2 vols. (Copenhagen: Jysk Arkaeologisk Selskabs Skrifter, 1976). Clonmacnoise Bridge: S. Duke, "Irish Bridge Sheds Light on Dark Ages," *Science* 10, 4 (1996), p. 480. The quotation about architecture is from C. B. McClendon, *The Origins of Medieval Architecture: Building in Europe, A.D. 600–900* (New Haven and London: Yale University Press, 2005), p. 1.

2 The Decline of the Roman Empire

Details about Roman history can be found in the volumes of *The Cambridge Ancient History,* published by Cambridge University Press (New York and Cambridge). A valuable summary for western and central Europe is H. U. Nuber, "Das Römische Reich (260–476 n. Chr.)," in M. Geiberger et al., eds., *Imperium Romanum: Römer, Christen, Alamannen—Die Spätantike am Oberrhein* (Karlsruhe: Badisches Landesmuseum, 2005), pp. 12–25. Recent overviews are P. Heather, *The Fall of the Roman Empire* (New York: Oxford University Press, 2006), and B. Ward-Perkins, *The Fall of Rome and the End of Civilization* (New York: Oxford University Press, 2005). On particular parts of Europe, see M. Kulikowski, *Rome's Gothic Wars: From the Third Century to Alaric* (New York: Cambridge University Press, 2007), L. Wamser, ed., *Die Römer zwischen Alpen und Nordmeer* (Mainz: Philipp von Zabern, 2000), K. Dark, *Britain and the End of the Roman Empire* (Stroud: Tempus, 2000), and S. Esmond Cleary, *The End of Roman Britain* (London: Routledge and Kegan Paul, 1989). The quotations from Jordanes and Priscus are from C. D. Gordon, *The Age of Attila* (Ann Arbor: University of Michigan Press, 1960), pp. 61, 95. Other important discussions are J. H. W. G. Liebeschuetz, *Decline and Fall of the Roman City* (New York: Oxford University Press, 2001), and W. Pohl, "The Politics of Change: Reflections on the Transformation of the Roman World," in W. Pohl and M. Diesenberger, eds., *Integration und Herrschaft: Ethnische Identitäten und soziale Organisation im Frühmittelalter* (Vienna: Österreichische Akademie der Wissenschaften, 2002), pp. 275–88.

3 The Peoples of Europe

An excellent overview is H. Wolfram, *The Roman Empire and Its Germanic Peoples*, trans. by T. Dunlap (Berkeley: University of California Press, 1997). On Greek and Roman ideas about barbarians, D. Timpe, "Ethnologische Begriffsbildung in der Antike," in H. Beck, ed., *Germanenprobleme in heutiger Sicht* (Berlin and New York: Walter de Gruyter, 1986), pp. 22–40. Catalogues of recent exhibitions provide good discussion of specific peoples: on the Alamanni, *Die Alamannen* (Stuttgart: Archäologisches Landesmuseum Baden-Württemberg, 1997); on the Franks, *Die Franken: Wegbereiter Europas* (Mainz: von Zabern, 1996); on the Goths, *I Goti* (Milan: Electa, 1994); on the Huns, A. Koch, ed., *Attila und die Hunnen* (Speyer: Historisches Museum der Pfalz, 2007).

Recent literature on the problem of migrations includes S. Burmeister, "Archaeology and Migration: Approaches to an Archaeological Proof of Migration," *Current Anthropology* 41, 4 (2000), pp. 539–67; W. Pohl, *Die Völkerwanderung: Eroberung und Integration* (Stuttgart: W. Kohlahmmer, 2002); and A. S. Christensen, *Cassiodorus, Jordanes, and the History of the Goths: Studies in a Migration Myth* (Copenhagen: Museum Tusculanum Press, University of Copenhagen, 2002).

On Anglo-Saxons, see S. Lucy, *The Anglo-Saxon Way of Death: Burial Rites in Early England* (Stroud: Sutton, 2000), C. Hills, *The Origins of the English* (London: Duckworth, 2003), and F. Pryor, *Britain A.D.: A Quest for Arthur, England and the Anglo-Saxons* (London: HarperCollins, 2004). Migrations into eastern Europe: F. Daim, ed., *Reitervölker aus dem Osten: Hunnen + Awaren* (Eisenstadt: Burgenländische Landesregierung, 1996). Artificial skull deformation: P. Schröter, "Zur beabsichtigten künstlichen Kopfumformung im völkerwanderungszeitlichen Mitteleuropa," in H. Dannheimer and H. Dopsch, eds., *Die Bajuwaren von Severin bis Tassilo 488–788* (Munich: Freistaat Bayern, 1988), pp. 258–65. On the ways of life of the inhabitants of different parts of Europe, see M. Todd, *The Early Germans,* 2d ed. (Malden, Mass.: Blackwell, 2004), C. Thomas, *Celtic Britain* (New York: Thames and Hudson, 1986), and P. M. Barford, *The Early Slavs: Culture and Society in Early Medieval Eastern Europe* (Ithaca, N.Y.: Cornell University Press, 2001). The quotation from Gildas is from *Britain A.D.* (above), p. 125. The spread of Christianity: K. Hopkins, *A World Full of Gods: Pagans, Jews, and Christians in the Roman Empire* (London: Weidenfeld & Nicolson, 1999), P. R. L. Brown, *The Rise of Western Christendom: Triumph and Diversity, A.D. 200–1000* (Malden, Mass.: Blackwell, 2003), and M. Carver, ed., *The Cross Goes North: Processes of Conversion in Northern Europe, AD 300–1300* (Rochester, N.Y.: Boydell and Brewer, 2003). On long-distance connections, see A. Harris, *Byzantium, Britain and the West: The Archaeology of Cultural Identity AD 400–650* (Stroud: Tempus, 2003). Jordanes's description of Attila's funeral is from C. C. Mierow, *The Gothic History of Jordanes,* 2d ed. (Princeton: Princeton University Press, 1915), pp. 124–25. For a recent discussion of Sutton Hoo, see M. Carver, *Sutton Hoo: Burial Ground of Kings?* (Philadelphia: University of Pennsylvania Press, 1998).

The standard study of the new art style is G. Haseloff, *Die germanische Tierornamentik in der Völkerwanderungszeit,* 3 vols. (Berlin and New York: Walter de Gruyter, 1981). The quotation about Charlemagne's dress comes from Einhard, *Vita Karoli Magni: The Life of Charlemagne,* trans. by E. S. Firchow and E. H. Zeydel (Dudweiler: AQ-Verlag, 1985), p. 89.

4 Childeric and Other Early Dark Age Kings

The literature on the Childeric grave is immense. Good introductions are G. Halsall, "Childeric's Grave, Clovis' Succession, and the Origins of the Merovingian Kingdom," in R. W. Mathisen and D. Shanzer, eds., *Society and Culture in Late Antique Gaul* (Aldershot: Ashgate, 2001), pp. 116–33, and B. Young, "Tomb of Childeric," in P. Bogucki and P. J. Crabtree, eds., *Ancient Europe 8000 B.C.–A.D. 1000: Encyclopedia of the Barbarian World* (New York: Thomson/Gale, 2004), vol. 2, pp. 519–24. On the recent excavations at the site, see R. Brulet, "La sépulture du roi Childéric à Tournai et le site funéraire," in F. Vallet and M. Kazanski, eds., *La noblesse romaine et les chefs barbares du IIIe au VIIe siècle* (Paris: Musée des Antiquités Nationales, 1995), pp. 309–26. My reconstruction of the funeral is based on F. Theuws and J. L. Nelson, eds., *Rituals of Power: From Late Antiquity to the Early Middle Ages* (Boston: Brill, 2000), and on what we know about other funeral ceremonies during that period in Europe, such as Attila's, the funeral depicted in *Beowulf,* and the archaeology of the Sutton Hoo grave. Apahida: K. Horedt and D. Protase, "Das zweite Fürstengrab von Apahida (Siebenbürgen)," *Germania* 50 (1972), pp. 174–220. The other rich graves of this group are discussed in J. Werner, "Der goldene Armring des Frankenkönigs Childerich und die germanischen Handgelenkringe der jüngeren Kaiserzeit," *Frühmittelalterliche Studien* 14 (1980), pp. 1–41, and, more recently, in Koch (chapter 3).

5 What Happened to the Roman Cities?

Roman Regensburg: K. Dietz et al., *Regensburg zur Römerzeit* (Regensburg: Friedrich Pustet, 1979). There are a great many books about the Roman Empire. Those by Heather and Ward-Perkins, cited above (chapter 1), are good places to find bibliographies of works about special topics. Population estimates for Roman Britain: D. Mattingly, *An Imperial Possession: Britain in the Roman Empire, 54 BC–AD 409* (New York: Allen Lane, 2006). On the city of Rome, see N. Christie, "Lost Glories? Rome at the End of Empire," in J. Coulston and H. Dodge, eds., *Ancient Rome: The Archaeology of the Eternal City* (Oxford: Oxford University School of Archaeology, 2000), pp. 306–31. Cologne: N. Aten, "Römische bis neuzeitliche Befunde der Ausgrabung auf dem Heumarkt in Köln," *Kölner Jahrbuch* 34 (2001), pp. 623–700. Mainz: H. Cüppers, ed., *Die Römer in Rheinland-Pfalz* (Stuttgart: Konrad Theiss, 1990). Isis and Mater Magna sanctuary in Mainz: M. Witteyer, *The Sanctuary of Isis and Mater Magna* (Mainz: von Zabern, 2004). Boats from the Mainz Hilton: B. Pferdehirt, *Das Museum für antike Schiffahrt* (Mainz: Römisch-Germanisches Zentralmuseum, 1995). On continuity of urban life, see B. Hårdh and L. Larsson, eds., *Central Places in the Migration and Merovingian Periods* (Lund: Department of Archaeology and Ancient History, 2002).

6 From Roman Londinium to Saxon Lundenwic: Continuity and Change (A.D. 43–800)

J. Hall and R. Merrifield, *Roman London* (London: Museum of London, 2000), is a well-illustrated little book that provides a fine introduction. More detail is provided in A. Vince, *Saxon London* (London: Seaby, 1990), I. Haynes et al., eds., *London Under Ground: The Archaeology of a City* (Oxford: Oxbow Books, 2000), C. Thomas, editor, *London's Archaeological Secrets: A World City Revealed* (London: Museum of London, 2003), and R. Cowie, "The Evidence for Royal Sites in Middle Anglo-Saxon London," *Medieval Archaeology* 48 (2004), pp. 201–9. On the Thames River, see J. Schneer, *The Thames* (New Haven: Yale University Press, 2005). Spitalfields graves: *The Spitalfields Roman*, 2d ed. (London: Museum of London, 2001). Lives of the people: A. Werner, *London Bodies: The Changing Shape of Londoners from Prehistoric Times to the Present Day* (London: Museum of London, 1998). On the tablet that documents the sale of a slave, see R. S. O. Tomlin, "'The Girl in Question': A New Text from Roman London," *Britannia* 34 (2003), pp. 41–51. Walbrook finds:

R. Merrifield, "Roman Metalwork from the Walbrook—Rubbish, Ritual or Redundancy?" *Transactions of the London and Middlesex Archaeological Society* 46 (1995), pp. 27–44. Temple of Mithras: J. D. Shepherd, *The Temple of Mithras, London* (London: English Heritage, 1998). Evidence for changes in the late Roman period: B. Watson, ed., *Roman London: Recent Archaeological Work, Journal of Roman Archaeology* Supplementary Series, no. 24 (Portsmouth, R.I., 1998).

7 New Centers in the North

These quotations (in my translations from the German) from the biography of Ansgar are from pp. 41, 43 (first quotation) and pp. 59, 61 (second quotation) in R. Buchner, ed., *Ausgewählte Quellen zur deutschen Geschichte des Mittelalters,* vol. 11, Rimbert, *Vita Anskarii,* trans. by W. Trillmich (Berlin: Rütten & Loenig, 1961). On Gudme, see P. O. Nielsen, K. Randsborg, and H. Thrane, eds., *The Archaeology of Gudme and Lundeborg* (Copenhagen: Akademisk Forlag, 1994). On the great hall there, K. K. Michaelsen and P. Ø. Sørensen, "En kongsgård fra jernalderen," *Årbog for Svendborg & Omegns Museum* (1993), pp. 24–35. On Helgö, see chapter 9. All of the sites mentioned here are discussed in H. Clarke and B. Ambrosiani, *Towns in the Viking Age,* rev. ed. (New York: St. Martin's Press, 1995).

8 The Revolution in the Countryside

The quotation at the start is from A. R. Benham, *English Literature from Widsith to the Death of Chaucer* (New Haven: Yale University Press, 1916), p. 26. Fundamental to this discussion is L. White, *Medieval Technology and Social Change* (New York: Oxford University Press, 1962). Recent treatments of the issues are R. Friedel, *A Culture of Improvement: Technology and the Western Millennium* (Cambridge, Mass.: MIT Press, 2007), and J. Mokyr, *Twenty-Five Centuries of Technological Change* (New York: Harwood Academic Publishers, 1990). Brebières: P. Demolon, *Le village mérovingien de Brebières, VIe–VIIe siècles* (Arras: Commission départementale des monuments historiques du Pas-De-

Calais, 1972). Vorbasse: S. Hvass, "Eine Dorfsiedlung während des 1. Jts. n. Chr. in Mitteljütland, Dänemark," *Bericht der Römisch-Germanischen Kommission* 67 (1986), pp. 529–42. Diet and food preparation: U. Gross, "Die Ernährung," in *Die Franken* (chapter 3), pp. 668–71, and M. Rösch, "Ackerbau und Ernährung," in *Die Alamannen* (chapter 3), pp. 323–30. Berinsfield cemetery study: K. L. Privat et al., "Stable Isotope Analysis of Human and Faunal Remains from the Anglo-Saxon Cemetery at Berinsfield, Oxfordshire: Dietary and Social Implications," *Journal of Archaeological Science* 29 (2002), pp. 779–90. Heights in southwestern Germany: J. Wahl et al., "Zwischen Masse und Klasse: Alamannen im Blickfeld der Anthropologie," in *Die Alamannen* (chapter 3), pp. 337–48. Heights in Denmark: B. J. Sellevold et al., *Iron Age Man in Denmark* (Copenhagen: Kongelige Nordiske Oldskriftselskab, 1984). On law systems, see Smith and Wickham books (chapter 1).

9 Crafting Tools and Ornaments for the New Societies

The quotation about Eligius is from H. Roth, *Kunst und Handwerk im frühen Mittelalter* (Stuttgart: Konrad Theiss, 1986), p. 9 (my translation from the German). Helgö: W. Holmqvist, ed., *Excavations at Helgö IV: Workshop, Part I,* and *Excavations at Helgö XII: Building Groups 1, 4, and 5* (Stockholm: KVHAA, 1972 and 1994). For other centers, see B. Hårdh and L. Larsson, eds., *Central Places in the Migration and Merovingian Periods* (Lund: Department of Archaeology and Ancient History, 2002). Runder Berg: H. Steuer, "Herrschaft von der Höhe," in *Die Alamannen* (chapter 1), pp. 149–62. Poysdorf grave: F. Daim and M. Mehofer, "Poysdorf," in *Reallexikon der germanischen Alterumskunde* 23 (2003), pp. 327–31. Grave at Kunszentmárton: J. Werner, "Zur Verbreitung frühgeschichtlicher Metallarbeiten (Werkstatt-Wanderhandwerk-Handel-Familienverbindung)," *Early Medieval Studies* I (Antikvariskt Arkiv 38) (1970), pp. 65–81.

10 Royal Exchange and Everyday Trade

The two quotations are from pp. 52, 53 of S. Allott, *Alcuin of York—His Life and Letters* (York: William Session, 1974). Tintagel: C. Thomas, *Book of*

Tintagel: Arthur and Archaeology (London: Batsford, 1993). The Dorestad excavations appear in W. A. van Es and W. J. H. Verwers, *Excavations at Dorestad: The Harbour: Hoogstraat I* (Amersfoort: Rijksdienst voor het Oudheidkundig Bodemonderzoek, 1980). On other trade centers of northern Europe, see *Central Places,* cited above (chapter 9). The Nydam boat: F. Rieck, "The Ships from Nydam Bog," in L. Jørgensen et al., eds., *The Spoils of Victory: The North in the Shadow of the Roman Empire* (Copenhagen: National Museum, 2003), pp. 296–309.

The main publication of the Sutton Hoo find is R. Bruce-Mitford, *The Sutton Hoo Ship-Burial,* 3 vols. (London: British Museum, 1975–83). A much shorter and less technically detailed version by the same author is *The Sutton Hoo Ship-Burial: A Handbook* (London: British Museum, 2d ed., 1972). Trade in this period: T. Pestell and K. Ulmschneider, eds., *Markets in Early Medieval Europe: Trading and 'Productive' Sites, 650–850* (Bollington: Windgather Press, 2003). Coptic bowl quantity estimates: H. Steuer, *Frühgeschichtliche Sozialstrukturen in Mitteleuropa* (Göttingen: Vandenhoeck & Ruprecht, 1982). Danish king's thirteenth-century law on treasure: O. Klindt-Jensen, *A History of Scandinavian Archaeology,* trans. by G. R. Poole (London: Thames and Hudson, 1975), p. 9. On treasure in general during this period: M. Hardt, "Royal Treasures and Representation in the Early Middle Ages," in W. Pohl and H. Reimitz, eds., *Strategies of Distinction: The Construction of Ethnic Communities, 300–800* (Boston: Brill, 1998), pp. 255–80. Pietroasa: E. Dunareanu-Vulpe, *Der Schatz von Pietroasa* (Bucharest: Meridiane, 1967). Discussion of the evidence of the distribution of garnet and implications for understanding political protection and peace: B. Arrhenius, *Merovingian Garnet Jewellery: Emergence and Social Implications* (Stockholm: Almqvist & Wiksell, 1985).

11 Spread of the New Religion

The quotation is from p. 68 of R. P. C. Hanson, *The Life and Writings of the Historical Saint Patrick* (New York: Seabury Press, 1983). Also on St. Patrick, see C. Bourke, *Patrick: The Archaeology of a Saint* (Belfast: Ulster Museum, 1993). On Ulfilas, see Heather (chapter 1), pp. 76–80. On early Christianity, see sources cited in chapter 1. Woman's grave under the Cologne Cathedral: O. Doppelfeld, "Das fränkische Frauengrab unter dem Chor des Kölner Doms," *Germania* 38 (1960), pp. 89–113. Ornamental pattern on the fibulae: C. von Carnap-Bornheim, "Zoomorphes Cloisonné auf dem Bügelfibelpaar aus dem Frauengrab unter dem Kölner Dom," *Archäologisches Korrespondenzblatt* 26 (1996), pp. 507–16. On style and decoration as indicative of new political units forming, see L. Hedeager, "Migration Period Europe: The Formation of a Political Mentality," in *Rituals of Power* (chapter 4), pp. 15–57. On religious interpretation of the new styles, see N. Wicker, "The Scandinavian Animal Styles in Response to Mediterranean and Christian Narrative Art," in *The Cross Goes North* (chapter 3), pp. 531–50. Hinton St. Mary mosaic: J. M. C. Toynbee, "A New Roman Mosaic Pavement Found in Dorset," *Journal of Roman Studies* 54 (1964), pp. 7–14. Hoxne hoard: R. Bland and C. Johns, *The Hoxne Treasure: An Illustrated Introduction* (London: British Museum, 1993). Wittislingen fibula: J. Werner, *Das alamannische Fürstengrab von Wittislingen* (Munich: C. H. Beck, 1950). Naab-Danube water deposits: K. Spindler, "Gewässerfunde," in S. Rieckhoff-Pauli and W. Torbrügge, eds., *Regensburg-Kelheim-Straubing*, part 1 (Stuttgart: Konrad Theiss, 1984), pp. 212–23. Swords in the Thames: D. M. Wilson, "Some Neglected Late Anglo-Saxon Swords," *Medieval Archaeology* 9 (1965), pp. 32–54. Oberdorla: G. Behm-Blancke, "Die germanische Kultstätte von Oberdorla," in J. Herrmann, ed., *Archäologie in der Deutschen Demokratischen Republik*, vol. 1 (Stuttgart: Konrad Theiss, 1989), pp. 174–76. On the site of Tara, see B. Raftery, *Pagan Celtic Ireland* (New York: Thames and Hudson, 1994). On Le Puy, Bonn, and Uley, see R. Merrifield, *The Archaeology of Ritual and Magic* (New York: New Amsterdam, 1987). Water Newton: K. S. Painter, "The Water Newton Silver: Votive or Liturgical?" *Journal of the British Archaeological Association* 152 (1999), pp. 1–23.

12 Arts, Scholarship, and Education

This quotation comes from p. 93 of the book about Charlemagne cited for chapter 3. On metalwork, see Roth (chapter 9). The Donzdorf fibula: E. M. Neuffer, *Der Reihengräberfeld von Donzdorf* (Stuttgart: Müller and Gräff, 1972). On the Sutton Hoo helmet, see the works cited by Bruce-Mitford (chapter 10). Ardagh Chalice: S. Youngs, *'The Work of Angels': Masterpieces of Celtic Metalwork, 6th–9th Centuries AD* (Austin: University of Texas Press, 1990). On book illumination, see H. Pulliam, *Word and Image in the Book of Kells* (Dublin: Four Courts Press, 2006), and G. Henderson, *From Durrow to Kells: The Insular Gospel-Books, 650–800* (New York: Thames and Hudson, 1987).

Books, scholarship, writing, illumination, and education on the continent are discussed in *The Civilization of Charlemagne* (chapter 1). Lindisfarne: M. P. Brown, *Painted Labyrinth: The World of the Lindisfarne Gospels* (London: British Library, 2003). Architecture: McClendon, cited in chapter 1. Irish missions to Britain and the continent are discussed in C. Thomas (chapter 1). For Bede, see Goffart (chapter 1), and for Alcuin, see S. Allott, *Alcuin of York, c. A.D. 732 to 804: His Life and Letters* (York: William Sessions, 1974).

13 Charlemagne's Elephant and the History of Europe

My discussion is based on R. Hodges, "Charlemagne's Elephant," *History Today* 50, 12 (2000), pp. 21–27, reprinted in R. Hodges, *Goodbye to the Vikings? Re-Reading Early Medieval Archaeology* (London: Duckworth, 2006), pp. 72–79.

Acknowledgments

❖

MANY INDIVIDUALS PROVIDED INSPIRATION, ADVICE, hospitality, and publications to assist with the writing of this book. Jack Repcheck, my editor at W. W. Norton, was, as always, a source of excellent advice and encouragement at all stages of preparation, writing, and revising. His assistant, Mikael Awake, was very helpful with quick and clear answers to my many questions.

Other people whose help and advice I wish to acknowledge include Eric Bangs, Ton Derks, Bernd Engelhardt, Heather Flowers, Lotte Hedeager, J. D. Hill, Richard Hingley, Henrik Jansen, Kristina Jennbert, Hayley Jirasek, Lars Larsson, Christopher Morris, Oliver Nicholson, Nico Roymans, Peter Schröter, Phillip Sellew, John Soderberg, Berta Stjernquist, Bernard Wailes, and Willem Willems.

Support for the research upon which this book is based

was provided by the University of Minnesota's Department of Anthropology, Graduate School, and Office of International Programs. I thank all three units for their assistance.

As always, the staff of the Interlibrary Loan office of the University of Minnesota library was extremely helpful in securing resources that I needed from libraries throughout the United States and Europe.

My wife, Joan, and my sons, Chris and Nick, accompanied me on many of the trips during which I collected information and photographs for this book. They provided the best possible company, as well as inspiration. I dedicate this book to them and to the other members of my family.

Illustration Credits

❖

If not otherwise indicated, photographs are by the author.

Figure 3.2. From *A Guide to the Anglo-Saxon and Foreign Teutonic Antiquities* (British Museum, 1923), p. 9, Fig. 4. Reproduced with the permission of the Trustees of the British Museum.

Figures 4.1, 4.2, 4.3, 4.4. From Special Collections and Rare Books, University of Minnesota.

Figure 6.5. Copyright Peter Froste / Museum of London.

Figure 8.1. From John Haywood, *The Penguin Historical Atlas of the Vikings* (London: Viking, 1995), pp. 36–37. Text copyright John Haywood; design and maps copyright Swanston Publishing Ltd. Reproduced by permission of Penguin Books Ltd.

Figure 9.1. From *A Guide to the Anglo-Saxon and Foreign Teutonic Antiquities* (London: British Museum, 1923), p. 30, Fig. 22. Reproduced with the permission of the Trustees of the British Museum.

Figure 10.2. Photo by Gabriel Hildebrand / Museum of National Antiquities, Stockholm, Sweden.

Figure 12.2. Landesmuseum Württemberg; Peter Frankenstein, Hendrik Zwietasch.

Index

❖

Page numbers in *italics* refer to illustrations and maps.